Layman's Bible Book Commentary
Hosea, Joel, Amos, Obadiah, Jonah

LAYMAN'S BIBLE BOOK COMMENTARY

HOSEA, JOEL, AMOS, OBADIAH, JONAH
VOLUME 13

Billy K. Smith

BROADMAN PRESS
Nashville, Tennessee

© Copyright 1982 ● Broadman Press.

All rights reserved.

4211-83

ISBN: 0-8054-1183-6

Dewey Decimal Classification: 224.6

Subject heading: BIBLE. O.T. MINOR PROPHETS

Library of Congress Catalog Card Number: 80-68536

Printed in the United States of America

Foreword

The *Layman's Bible Book Commentary* in twenty-four volumes was planned as a practical exposition of the whole Bible for lay readers and students. It is based on the conviction that the Bible speaks to every generation of believers but needs occasional reinterpretation in the light of changing language and modern experience. Following the guidance of God's Spirit, the believer finds in it the authoritative word for faith and life.

To meet the needs of lay readers, the *Commentary* is written in a popular style, and each Bible book is clearly outlined to reveal its major emphases. Although the writers are competent scholars and reverent interpreters, they have avoided critical problems and the use of original languages except where they were essential for explaining the text. They recognize the variety of literary forms in the Bible, but they have not followed documentary trails or become preoccupied with literary concerns. Their primary purpose was to show what each Bible book meant for its time and what it says to our own generation.

The Revised Standard Version of the Bible is the basic text of the *Commentary*, but writers were free to use other translations to clarify an occasional passage or sharpen its effect. To provide as much interpretation as possible in such concise books, the Bible text was not printed along with the comment.

Of the twenty-four volumes of the *Commentary*, fourteen deal with Old Testament books and ten with those in the New Testament. The volumes range in pages from 140 to 168. Four major books in the Old Testament and five in the New are treated in one volume each. Others appear in various combinations. Although the allotted space varies, each Bible book is treated as a whole to reveal its basic message with some passages getting special attention. Whatever plan of Bible study the reader may follow, this *Commentary* will be a valuable companion.

Despite the best-seller reputation of the Bible, the average survey of Bible knowledge reveals a good deal of ignorance about it and its primary meaning. Many adult church members seem to think that its study is intended for children and preachers. But some of the newer translations have been making the Bible more readable for all ages. Bible study has branched out from Sunday into other days of the week, and into neighborhoods rather than just in churches. This *Commentary* wants to meet the growing need for insight into all that the Bible has to say about God and his world and about Christ and his fellowship.

BROADMAN PRESS

Contents

HOSEA

JOEL

AMOS

OBADIAH

JONAH

HOSEA

Introduction

The Book of Hosea stands first in the Book of the Twelve, known also as the Minor Prophets. Hosea was one of four eighth-century BC prophets who ministered to God's people in Israel and Judah. Amos and Hosea served the Northern Kingdom of Israel, while Isaiah and Micah ministered to the Southern Kingdom of Judah. This quartet of men represents the beginning of the classical, or writing, prophets.

The Prophet

The superscription names Hosea as a recipient of God's word. The language used is a typical description of prophetic reception of God's revelation. The English name "Hosea" occurs only four times in the entire Bible (1:1, once; 1:2, twice; Rom. 9:25, once). The last king of Israel bore the same name, but it is spelled "Hoshea" rather than "Hosea." Joshua's name at first was Hoshea. "Hosea" means salvation, the urgent need of Hosea's family and his nation.

Hosea's father was named "Beeri," a word meaning "my spring." This name probably represents the parents' joy at the birth of a son through whom the clan would continue as a living spring of water.

The only other personal information about Hosea in the superscription is the date of his ministry during the reigns of certain kings in Judah (Uzziah, Jotham, Ahaz, and Hezekiah) and in Israel (Jeroboam II). Judean kings listed in the superscription to the Book of Isaiah match this Judean list exactly. Perhaps the writer would alert the reader with this list that Hosea and Isaiah were contemporaries. Added together, the Judean kings' reigns cover a period of approximately one hundred years, from the beginning of Uzziah's reign, 783 BC, to the close of Hezekiah's time in office, 687 BC. Jeroboam II reigned in Israel from 786 to 746 BC. Internal evidence

11

suggests that Hosea began to minister before the close of Jeroboam II's reign (about 750 BC) and continued to near the end of Hoshea's reign (about 725 BC).

Hosea was a native of Israel. His concern was with Israel. Most place names mentioned are in Israel. He seems to have had personal knowledge of the religious and political conditions in Israel. He must have included himself when he referred to "our king" in an address to Israel.

The Times

The period represented by Uzziah's reign in Judah (783 to 740 BC) and Jeroboam II's reign in Israel (786 to 746 BC) was marked by peace and prosperity for both nations. Hosea began to minister toward the close of Jeroboam's reign. His call to prophetic ministry came as he approached the age for marriage. The Lord ordered him to take "a wife of harlotry" and "have children of harlotry." These terms reflect the tenor of the times. Jezreel, Hosea's first child, became a walking message of judgment upon the house of Jehu (1:4). Jeroboam II, Jehu's great-grandson, represented that house as the current king in Israel. But Jezreel symbolized the end of Jehu's dynasty. Fulfillment came when Zechariah, Jeroboam II's son, was assassinated after only six months as Israel's king. His was the first of a series of political assassinations.

The first period of Hosea's ministry coincided with the last four or five years of Jeroboam II's reign. His marriage to Gomer and the birth of his children are associated with that time frame. Chapters 1—3 reflect this era of peace.

A second major period of Hosea's prophetic activity was linked with Tiglath-pileser III's (popularly known as Pul) rise to the throne of Assyria in 745 BC. He forced Menahem, king of Israel, to pay a heavy tribute. Menahem's son, Pekahiah, succeeded him, but Pekah murdered Pekahiah and formed an anti-Assyrian coalition. The Syro-Ephraimitic war against Judah was part of this venture. Hoshea murdered Pekah, surrendered to Assyria, paid tribute, and ascended Israel's throne as a vassal of Tiglath-pileser. Chapters 4—8 echo the political intrigue of this erratic period in Israel's history.

The third period of Hosea's proclamation was associated with the relative quiet brought on by Hoshea's surrender to Assyria. Chapters 9—12 reflect this time of "quiet before the storm." But when Shalmaneser V succeeded Tiglath-pileser III as king of Assyria in

727 BC, Hoshea withheld tribute. Chapters 13—14 reveal the tragic consequences of Israel's revolt.

The Marriage

How to interpret Hosea's marriage is not a settled issue. Yet everywhere in the book the marriage theme is evident. It dominates chapters 1 through 3 and surfaces now and again throughout chapters 4—14. Three large categories of interpretation cover most of the views: (1) The marriage is an allegory of the relationship between Yahweh and Israel; (2) The narrative presents the marriage experiences of the prophet as he understood them later; and (3) The prophet married a sacred prostitute as Yahweh ordered him to do.

Very few contemporary studies of Hosea accept the allegorical view of his marriage. Most maintain that Hosea actually married Gomer, but disagree over when she became unchaste. Thus, some fall into the second category and some into the third category mentioned above. All agree that Hosea's marriage had a profound effect on his ability to perceive the character of Israel's God.

The Book

The Book of Hosea falls into two major divisions. Chapters 1—3 contain mostly biographical and autobiographical materials. Chapters 4—14 consist of a collection of Hosea's oracles. Israel's guilt before God dominates chapters 4—8. Israel's punishment is announced in chapters 9—11. Guilt, punishment, and hope are combined in chapters 12—14.

Love: The Cement of Family Relationships
1:1 to 3:5

The Title (1:1)

The heading identifies the nature of the materials contained in the Book of Hosea. It gives the prophet's source of authority, his name, his father's name, and his period of activity as a prophet. Both the personal materials in chapters 1—3 and the oracles in chapters 4—14 are "word of the Lord." All of the book is word of the Lord. "Word" is singular, not plural. The singular form signifies the uniform will of God expressed in a variety of materials. These collected words of Hosea are God's word and should be read as such.

Hosea's authority for prophetic ministry was grounded in the fact that the word of the Lord came to him. He did not produce the word. It "came," or happened to him as an event of revelation.

The title reflects more interest in Hosea's time than in his person. Judean kings are listed first, though Hosea ministered in Israel. Then only one Israelite king, Jeroboam II, is named. Internal evidence indicates that Hosea's period of ministry extended far beyond the reign of Jeroboam II (786-746 BC). Why no other Israelite king is named remains a mystery. For about twenty-five years (750-724 BC), Hosea ministered to a nation in sharp decline. Israel fell to the Assyrians in 721 BC when Sargon II successfully completed the siege begun by Shalmaneser V.

The Prophet's Family and God's Family (1:2-9)

The narrative about Hosea's marriage to Gomer and the three children born to them is not biography. It is prophetic symbolism. The chief interest is not in Hosea and his family, but in God and Israel. Hosea's four successive acts are "word of the Lord." The marriage symbolizes God's indictment against Israel. Their sin was religious faithlessness. The children's names are sentences of judgment because of that sin.

A repeated literary pattern ties these four prophetic actions together. The Lord commands the prophet to perform a specific act. Interpretation of the act, introduced by "for," follows the command. Prophetic obedience is reported after the first command and implied after the next three.

The first line of verse 2 functions as a title for verses 2-9. Septuagint translators took the verbal form rendered "spoke" in verse 2a to be a noun, "word." The full phrase is "the beginning of the word of the Lord to (by, or through) Hosea." Handled as a verbal form the title reads, "The beginning of the speaking of the Lord to (by, through) Hosea." The Lord's four commands (vv. 2-9) marked the first period of Hosea's prophetic ministry. His first public act as prophet was his marriage to Gomer (v. 3).

The word translated "the Lord" is the personal name of Israel's covenant God. Most modern commentaries take "Yahweh" to be the best way to handle the name. What Yahweh said to Hosea is in the form of a command. In fact, two imperatives set forth God's directive for Hosea. "Go, take to yourself a wife" is the usual expression for marriage.

The kind of woman God ordered Hosea to marry is not clear. "Wife of harlotry" probably does not mean a soliciting prostitute. Later use of "harlotry" in the Book of Hosea suggests that the term refers to falling away from Yahweh (4:12; 5:4). Thus, any woman from among rebellious Israel could qualify as a possible wife for Hosea. "Children of harlotry" simply means offspring from Hosea's marriage to such a woman. This interpretation is made explicit by references to conception and birth.

Hosea's marriage to "a wife of harlotry" is symbolic of Israel's spiritual infidelity. "The land" (v. 2) denotes the nation, not the ground. "Commits great harlotry" is an emphatic statement. A literal translation reads, "committing harlotry, the land commits harlotry." Specific reference may be to Israel's involvement in the cult of Baal. Worship of this Canaanite god of fertility included sexual rites based on sympathetic magic. Israel gave herself to the local Baals in return for their gifts through the fertility of the land. However, Yahweh's covenant with Israel made him her legitimate husband. Israel's worship of Baal cast her as a harlot. "By forsaking the Lord" is literally from under (after) Yahweh. Israel was no longer under Yahweh's control.

Hosea's obedience to God's command to marry a wife of harlotry was immediate. He raised no questions concerning the strange order. He "went" and "took" Gomer the daughter of Diblaim. His conduct matched God's will exactly. Implied in Hosea's action is that Gomer fit God's requirement and was Hosea's personal choice. The name "Gomer" has no known symbolic or allegorical meaning, one indication of the factual nature of Hosea's marriage. With an increasing economy of words, the narrator reports that Gomer conceived and bore Hosea a son. "Bore him a son" means that the child belonged to Hosea and it was born in wedlock.

Yahweh ordered Hosea to give his son a symbolic name. "Jezreel" would remind Israel of the village and the valley associated with Jehu's purge (2 Kings 9:14 ff.). The name means "Yahweh sows." The populace felt that God himself must have sown the valley of Jezreel, since it was so fertile and fruitful. Interpretation of the name is related to the bloodshed associated with that area. There Jehu wiped out the house of Omri, including Joram and Jezebel (2 Kings 9:24,33). The "blood of Jezreel" must refer to Jehu's revolt against the Omrides. Jehu established himself upon the throne of Israel by bloodletting.

Now the name of Hosea's newborn son bears God's message of judgment upon the house of Jehu. "For yet a little while" indicates that Jehu's house would soon be punished. "Punish" is the translation of a verb that means visit with a view toward evaluation and judgment. Jeroboam II sat on the throne of Israel as the representative of Jehu's house. Only a few years later the end of Jehu's house came when Zechariah, Jeroboam II's son, was assassinated. Also God threatened to "put an end to the kingdom of the house of Israel." Of the six kings who followed Jeroboam II, only Menahem died a natural death. The rest were assassinated. For all practical purposes kingship in Israel ended with the murder of Zechariah, the last representative of Jehu's line.

"And on that day" (v. 5) is typical language designating a future day of God's intervention in Israel's history. God pledged to "break the bow of Israel" in the historic battleground of Jezreel. Here Jehu committed unjust acts and here God's punishment would be experienced. "Bow" stands for Israel's military equipment. To "break the bow" would be to destroy Israel's military capabilities. Fulfillment of this prophecy came in 734 BC when Tiglath-pileser III reduced Israel to a helpless vassal state.

The narrator related the birth of a second child to Hosea and Gomer (v. 6) with terse language. A time lapse of two or three years is implied between the birth of their son, Jezreel, and the birth of their daughter, "Not pitied." No reference is made to Hosea in the birth announcement. This omission does not argue conclusively for another father than Hosea. In similar brief style God's name is missing from the command about naming the child. The word translated "pitied" is a verb meaning "be shown compassion." A noun built on the verb means "womb," suggesting either the natural love parents have for their children or the brotherly feeling of those born from the same womb. But the name preceded by the negative particle symbolizes the end of God's compassion. Interpretation of the daughter's name makes clear its application to "the house of Israel." Once God showed compassion to Israel. No longer would he do so.

The harsh withdrawal of divine compassion from Israel did not include Judah (v. 7). "House of Judah" is placed in an emphatic position in the original text. God's deliverance of Judah without military aid may refer to the Sennacherib crisis of 701 BC (2 Kings 19:32 ff.).

Gomer weaned "Not pitied," conceived, and bore a son (v. 8). This report follows the established pattern but is even more abbreviated than the previous account. Why the writer noted that Gomer conceived the third child after the second was weaned is not explained. A lapse of three or more years is the implied time between the two children. Perhaps the reference to time is meant to magnify God's patience and hope before issuing the third and final threat. Israel had time to return to God.

The name of the third child, "Not my people," is covenant terminology. "You are my people and I am your God" is the usual way God's relation to Israel in the covenant is stated (see Ex. 6:7; Lev. 26:12; Deut. 26:17-18). However, the sentence interpreting the child's name announces that the covenant is no longer in force. Covenant vocabulary is turned into a formula of divorce. The word for God in the final line is the same word Moses learned in his call experience (Ex. 3:14). The full formula here is "You are not my people and I am not your 'I AM' " (AT). Only in this final threat is direct address used. The prophet's family became a walking witness against Israel, God's family. They symbolized God's rejection of Israel.

Hope for Broken Family Relationships (1:10 to 2:1)

Grammatical construction marks these verses as a prophetic saying about the future. Yahweh announced his divorce from Israel (vv. 2-9). Here he projected a future day of remarriage. In verses 2-9 "Jezreel" stands for judgment. Here "Jezreel" speaks of restoration. The pattern of judgment (1:2-9) followed by salvation (1:10 to 2:1) is continued throughout this section (1—3).

Reference to an immeasurable increase in population is the first of three themes in this Jezreel oracle from Israel's covenant traditions

(v. 10). God promised numerous seed to the patriarchs (Gen. 12:2; 26:4; 28:14). Here Hosea announces a future day of fulfillment.

A second theme is the Exodus manner of thinking about Israel as sons of God (Ex. 4:22-23). Hosea's name for them is "Sons of the living God" (1:10). Hosea 11:1 has God calling Israel "my son." Jezreel may be the unnamed "place" where the names will be reversed. Their renewed life would spring from the living God.

A united Israel under one head is the substance of the third theme in this oracle (v. 11). The era of kingship in Israel was a period of conflict and separation. Judah and Israel united recalls the tribal federation prior to that time. "Go up from the land" may be a play on the name "Jezreel" (God sows). The meaning would be "grow up" and possess the land. "One head" is neither a king nor the Lord. It designates a uniting leader appointed by Judah and Israel to seal their union. The "day of Jezreel" may refer to a liberation battle in the valley of Jezreel (v. 11). If so, it serves as an antithesis to 1:5.

Hosea 2:1 refers to the Northern Kingdom, since the prophet addressed his messages to them. Hosea ordered the people of Israel to speak to the people of Judah with the signs of the new covenant, "My people," and of grace, "She has obtained pity." Thus, hostile Israel and Judah will be reconciled to each other.

Discipline for a Disobedient Family (2:2-13)

Legal language casts this oracle in the form of a court proceeding. Yahweh as husband appears in the role of plaintiff against Israel, his unfaithful wife. "Plead" is a legal term suggesting a controversy. Some interpreters prefer "accuse" instead of "plead." To raise complaints against the accused was the plaintiff's role. The Lord appealed to the children to enter the litigation. His purpose was not divorce, but reconciliation. "Children" refers to individual Israelites, not Hosea's children, while "mother" stands for the whole nation. Israel's "lovers" (v. 5) are the Canaanite gods.

The specific complaint against Israel is stated: "She is not my wife,/and I am not her husband" (v. 2). This statement has been identified as a divorce declaration. But such identity makes no sense in a proceeding aimed at recovery of the wife. The form of the complaint is like the declaration of the broken covenant between

God and Israel (1:9). Here marriage represents the covenant, and "harlotry" threatens the break up of the marriage.

Both "harlotry" and "adultery" may refer to marks of identity worn in the Baal cult (2:2). Such items as headbands, rings, and necklaces identified a woman as a prostitute, much as a veil did in the days of the patriarchs (Gen. 38:14). Israel is asked to put away everything that reminds her of her adultery.

Appeal for reform is followed by a warning (v. 3). Should Israel fail to strip away her harlot marks and adultery signs, God will strip Israel naked. Clothing the wife was the legal duty of the husband (Ex. 21:10). But if she persisted in pursuing her lovers, the husband had the right under ancient Oriental law to strip her naked and expel her. The wife is the land, and her stripping is the drought that leaves it unfruitful. Note should be taken that death by stoning or burning, a punishment usual for adultery (Gen. 38:24; Lev. 21:9; Deut. 22:23), is not mentioned.

The children who were called on to enter accusations against their mother are included in the mother's guilt (v. 4). Israelites became "children of harlotry" when corporate Israel turned to Baal. "No pity" recalls the name of Hosea's daughter, ties chapter 2 to chapter 1, and registers Yahweh's response to harlotrous children. Their mother's guilt is stated emphatically (v. 5). She has "played the harlot" and "acted shamefully." Her words are entered as evidence of her willful attitude. She determined to "go after" her lovers, contrary to ordinary practice. "Lovers" have been identified already as Canaanite gods. Jeremiah and Ezekiel followed Hosea in applying the term to substitutes for Yahweh. Israel thought Baal supplied her food and water, wool and wax, and oil and drink. Israel expected all that nourishes, protects, and gives pleasure in return for worshiping the Baals. She did not know that Yahweh was the giver of these gifts (v. 8).

Three "therefore" oracles express the Lord's response to Israel's faithlessness (2:6-8,9-13,14-15). Almost always "therefore" marks the shift from the proof of guilt to the threat of punishment. That is not the case here. Correction is the aim of Yahweh's actions. The language pictures God's personal intervention. He is the one who will fence up Israel's way with thorns. He will erect a stone wall so that Israel will not find the paths leading to her lovers. Reference is probably to the roads leading to the Baal sanctuaries.

The theme of seeking but not finding the lover belongs to the rituals of love and marriage (Song of Sol. 3:1-4). "Pursue" is an intensive verb (v. 7). "Seek" is a technical word for shrine visitation. The expressed desire of the wife to return to her first husband suggests that she had initiated a divorce. Israel's law would not allow the woman to return to her first husband (Deut. 24:1-4). However, here Israel's return to Yahweh is the point of concern. Her return would acknowledge that the past relationship with Yahweh was better than her present alliance with Baal. In ignorance Israel credited Yahweh's gifts of grain, wine, oil, and wealth to Baal. To add insult to injury, Israel used the most precious of Yahweh's gifts (gold) as offerings to Baal, or to make cult images.

The Lord's second action is to cut off his gifts to Israel (vv. 9-13). Drought is probably the instrument of privation. Without water the land would be fruitless. Israel would suffer need for food, clothing, and pleasure (v. 9). God's action would be public, "in the sight of her lovers," and, thus, more painful (v. 10). From God's viselike grip, Israel's lovers would be helpless to rescue her. Feasts in celebration of harvest would end.

What Israel thought to be her "hire" for services rendered to her "lovers," the Lord would turn into thickets and dens for wild animals (v. 12). Established feast days in worship of Yahweh had been prostituted by Israel as seasons for worship of Baal (v. 13). In hot pursuit of her lovers, Israel forgot God. "Forgot" is opposite to "know," or "acknowledge." What a sad commentary on Israel's fidelity to her covenant with Yahweh!

Initiative for a New Beginning (2:14-23)

The Lord's third action is aimed at renewal. God would renew his courtship of Israel (v. 14). Wilderness days came to be idealized as the honeymoon period in God's relationship to Israel. Back in that ideal setting, Yahweh would have Israel isolated from her "lovers." He would speak new, tender, heart-stirring words to her. Once more he would offer her "her vineyards" (v. 15). "Valley of Achor" means valley of trouble. There Achan and his family were put to death for Achan's sin (Josh. 7:16 ff.). God promised to give the Valley of Achor as the gateway to hope.

Renewal in the future day of salvation and under God's initiative will bring a number of gratifying results for Israel. Israel's renewed loyalty to God will be expressed by the removal of the name Baal from their vocabulary. No more will Baal and Yahweh be confused in worship (vv. 16-17).

Israel's new covenant with God will bring about peaceful and safe conditions similar to the beginning of time (v. 18). This new betrothal of Israel to Yahweh will result from God's initiative. It will be permanent, because the basis is the character of God (vv. 19-20). God's righteousness, justice, steadfast love, mercy, and faithfulness represent the bride-price. Pure grace will be the foundation of the new covenant. "Know" pictures the intimacy of Israel's new relationship to God.

The land's renewed fertility will be expressed by bountiful crops (vv. 21-22a). That fruitfulness would be God's "answer" to Israel's need. "Jezreel" must be the name of Israel whom God himself will "sow" in the renewed land (vv. 22b-23a). In judgment God scattered Israel (1:4 f.). In renewal he will sow them. The names of Hosea's children had been symbols of judgment and breach of God's covenant with Israel. But they will become symbols of the new covenant relationship between God and Israel.

Basis for Restored Relationships (3:1-5)

Love is the basis for Hosea's actions to restore his relationship to his adulterous wife. "Go" and "love" are commands from God to Hosea. Some interpreters question whether or not love can be commanded. God can do so because love does not mean "fall in love." Neither does it signify sexual intercourse, nor the legal act of marriage. Love, as Hosea uses it (11:1; 14:4), means a helping, healing relationship. It is the opposite of hatred (9:15). Here in verse 1, love is the husband's act of winning back the unfaithful wife. "Woman" here and "wife" in 1:2 come from the same word.

"Again," along with the application of the symbolism to Yahweh's relationship to Israel, suggests that Gomer is the unfaithful woman in question. She is described as "beloved of a paramour." This second use of love means lustful desire, since the woman is tabbed an adulteress. The love between her and the "paramour" (desired lover) is but a practice of adultery.

Notice that Hosea is to love "as the Lord loves." His love for his adulterous wife was to be patterned after God's love for wayward Israel. Love is the basis for restored relationships in both cases.

Hosea's actions were to be modeled after Yahweh's actions. If God could love "the people [sons] of Israel," even though they turned to other lovers (gods), then Hosea should be able to love his faithless wife. "Cakes of raisins" were eaten by participants in the ceremonial activities associated with worship (2 Sam. 6:19).

Hosea did what the Lord and love required (v. 2). He redeemed her. "Bought" suggests not only paying the required price, but also bargaining for his wife. This act made her Hosea's legal possession. The price paid was "fifteen shekels of silver" and about sixteen and a half bushels of barley. A "homer" was about eleven bushels and a "lethech" was half that amount. The value of the barley matched the value of the silver, giving a sum equal to thirty shekels of silver. That amount was the price of a slave (Ex. 21:32). This report suggests an actual event, that Hosea was not wealthy, and that his wife had become a slave as a result of her downward plunge into prostitution. Hosea's love was not a fickle emotion but a firm action.

The strength of Hosea's love was evident in the discipline imposed upon his wife and himself (v. 3). "Many days" means temporarily, not forever. The "afterward" of verse 5 indicates an end to the period of discipline. As God's judgment of Israel was temporary and served the purpose of renewal, so Hosea's restrictions were temporary and were aimed at restored relationships. "Dwell as mine" means stay at home with Hosea, resigned to household duties. There she would be protected from the temptation she could not resist. There she would have only Hosea's presence and words. Deprived of sexual activity, even with Hosea, she could consider restored relationships with Hosea undistracted.

Verse 4 contains the reason for Hosea's actions. They bore God's message to Israel. The nation will "dwell many days" under the discipline of God's love. They will be deprived of leadership: "king or prince." Ritual worship activity will cease, "without sacrifice or pillar." Usual ways of learning God's ways will be removed, "ephod or teraphim." Politically and religiously Israel will be reduced to wilderness conditions.

God's purpose in the temporary judgment is renewal (v. 5). "Afterward" means beyond the discipline of verse 4. Reduced to reliance on God by the removal of all substitutes, Israel will recognize God as redeemer and provider. "Return" is the technical term for repentance in the Old Testament. "Seek" is Hosea's word for futile visitation of the pagan sanctuaries (2:7). Here the goal of seeking is "the Lord," the God of the covenant. "Fear" means dread and trembling, or perhaps excitement. "His goodness" includes the natural resources of Palestine as well as God's faithfulness to Israel. So strong is God's love that he does what is impossible according to the law (Deut. 24:1 ff.). He brings home his faithless wife (Israel) who had legally come into another's possession. Love is neither cheap nor easy. But it is powerful and effective.

Love: The Requirement of Covenant Loyalty
4:1 to 6:11

God's Controversy with Israel (4:1-3)

Hosea's appeal to the people of Israel to "hear the word of the Lord" represents a new beginning. Already the entire Book of Hosea has been designated "the word of the Lord" (1:1). This second section of Hosea's sayings is God's word also. Three times in the first cycle the message has moved from threats of judgment to promises of salvation (chs. 1, 2, and 3 respectively). Now the introductory proclamation formula, "Hear the word of Lord," marks a fresh beginning.

The prophet appealed to the "people of Israel" to hear God's word. More interest centers around how one speaks than how one hears in the present generation. With the command to hear God's word, Hosea reflected the biblical emphasis on careful hearing and heeding of God's word. "Word of the Lord" is a technical phrase for divine revelation. "O people of Israel" is literally sons of Israel.

The term translated "controversy" is a legal word. Lawsuit might be a better translation to capture its court association. The writing prophets used the term metaphorically, not literally. God and Israel related to each other under a contract marked by covenant stipulations. Any breach of contract was the ground for one party to take the other covenant party into court. The language used here suggests that Israel had broken her agreement with God and that God was taking Israel to court.

The prophet leveled a threefold charge against "the inhabitants of the land" (v. 1b). The seriousness of the charge is heightened by the fact that Israel lived on the land God gave them, enjoyed its blessings, but failed to acknowledge God's ownership. Stated negatively, the charge includes "no faithfulness," "or kindness," and "no knowledge of God." The root meaning of the word translated *faithfulness* is to stay, to sustain, to support. It means to be firm. Sometimes the noun used here is translated truth. A thing is true because it is firm, dependable, or reliable. But precisely that quality was missing from covenant life in Israel.

No single English word is adequate to capture all the facets of the term translated "kindness." Proposed words include love, loving-kindness, steadfast love, and devotion. This term is uniquely related to covenant faithfulness. It may describe God's love for man, as well as man's love for God, his brother, or his neighbor. But always the frame of reference is the covenant.

The basic element missing in Israel's covenant life was "knowledge of God." Knowledge, as it is used in the Old Testament, is more experiential than intellectual. It is a warm, intimate term. Know is used to picture sexual intercourse between a husband and his wife (Gen. 4:1,17,25). Here "knowledge of God" means intimate knowledge of God's revealed will in the law (v. 1). Absence of that knowledge in Israel was proved by the presence of "swearing, lying, killing, stealing, and committing adultery."

The positive side to the prophet's charge against Israel includes five specific breaches of the law (v. 2). These are not unrelated to the negative part of the charge discussed above. Broken relationships between a man and his fellowman inevitably follow broken relationships between a man and his God. A man cannot be right with his brother until he gets right with God. Truth, love, and knowledge of God were missing in Israel. In their place were swearing (breach of the Third Commandment), lying (breach of the Ninth Commandment), killing (breach of the Sixth Commandment), stealing (breach of the Eighth Commandment), and committing adultery (breach of the Seventh Commandment). A literal translation of the last line in verse 2 reveals the excesses of God's people: "They break out and bloods touch bloods." A complete breakdown of morality characterized Israel.

"Therefore" usually introduces God's coming judgment. But some current situation for which Israel's sins are responsible may stand behind verse 3. Drought could bring on mourning and a loss of vitality for man, beast, bird, and fish. However, more than a local catastrophe would be required to produce the universal suffering described here. Earlier Hosea spoke of nature's share in Israel's restoration (2:18-21). Now he describes creation's participation in the curse brought on by Israel's covenant-breaking. All creation is adversely affected by mankind's sin. The land mourns. Its inhabitants become weak. Even the beasts and the birds languish and the fish are removed. How serious indeed is Israel's breach of covenant!

God's Case Against the Priests (4:4-10)

This passage is linked to the preceding verses by the words "contend" and "contention." God's controversy with the inhabitants of the land (vv. 1-3) is narrowed to the priests and the religious community (vv. 4-10). Hosea seems to be responding to an official protest against his announcement of judgment. His answer is subject to more than one interpretation. He may have meant that reproof was out of order since everyone was guilty. Or he may have been disparaging any effort at correction on the ground that no one would listen. This much is certain: God's complaint is against faithless religious leaders.

"O priest" probably refers to a high official in an important sanctuary, like Amaziah of Bethel (Amos 7:10), rather than to priests collectively. The third person plural references in verses 7-10 appear to include the priests as a group. "The prophet" is a person connected with the centers of worship who shared the corruption of Israel's religion along with the priest (v. 5). Both the priest and the prophet will "stumble" as a result of God's judgment upon them. The priest will stumble in the daylight when one would not normally stumble. The prophet will stumble in the night when prophets normally received nocturnal revelations. This is the only reference in Hosea to the prophet as a part of the religious establishment.

"Your mother" refers to the priest's mother, not the nation Israel. Judgment against the priest could include his family, as the similar judgment oracle in Amos illustrates (Amos 7:17). The word translated "destroy" may mean silence, though no reason is given for silencing the priest's mother.

"My people" designates Israel as God's people in a unique sense (v. 6). Israel's condition, "are destroyed," reflects the priest's guilt. The kind of verb used suggests that Israel's destruction is a completed action. God will destroy the priest's family because the priest's failure has destroyed God's family. "Lack of knowledge" is literally lack of *the* knowledge. The antecedent of "the knowledge" must be "knowledge of God" in verse 1.

Responsibility for Israel's lack of knowledge rested with the priest, since teaching the knowledge of God was his specific task. God charged the priest with rejecting the knowledge. Emphatic use of "you" underscores the gravity of the priest's failure. Use of the article with knowledge makes it definite. What the priest rejected was the knowledge of God. The word translated "rejected" may mean scorned also. A conscious negligence is implied.

The priest's crime is matched by God's judgment. He had rejected the knowledge of God. God would reject him as a priest. He had "forgotten" the law of God. God would forget his children. No longer would the priesthood be hereditary. "Forgotten" is more than a mental lapse. It includes a deliberate turning away from and forsaking someone (Isa. 49:14). "Law of your God" means the teaching, principles, or revelation of God. How could a priest forget God's instruction for life (Deut. 32:47)? To teach the law of God was his primary duty. Neglect of this duty made the priest responsible for the destruction of God's people.

Priests as a group are referred to indirectly in verses 7-10. God's charge against them is that their increase in number is matched by increased sin. Or the emphasis is upon the fact that all the priests sin against God. The exercise of power has a way of corrupting even religious people. The word translated "sinned" means to miss the mark. An increase in the number of priests serving God should have resulted in a decrease in sin. The opposite was true. God threatened to change their glory and honor into dishonor. "Their glory into shame" is placed ahead of the verb for emphasis.

The priest's portion of the sin offering became more important to the priest than the sinner's pardon (v. 8). The emphatic nature of verse 8 is reflected in a literal translation: "The sin [perhaps sin offering] of my people they eat and unto their iniquity they lift up their souls." What a vicious circle! The priest neglected to teach the law. The people plunged into sin. They brought more offerings. The priest's portion grew.

"Like people, like priest" means that the priest will suffer the same punishment as the people (v. 9). Notice that it is God who will visit his people and priests to punish them. The word translated "requite" means cause to return. "Ways" means life-style, or way of living. Like a boomerang, God will cause the priests' and the peoples' evil deeds to return upon them as punishment. Even excessive eating would not satisfy the priests' hunger. Neither would accelerated participation in the fertility cult increase their population (v. 10).

God's Indictment of Israel's Religion (4:11-14)

"Harlotry" is the sin that links verses 11-14 with verses 4-10. To "cherish harlotry" is set over against forsaking the Lord in verse 10. Led away by "a spirit of harlotry" is set over against leaving their God in verse 12. The oracle begins and ends with related wisdom sayings (vv. 11, 14c). "Understanding" in verse 11 is "heart," the seat of will and intellect in Hebrew thought. "Understanding" in verse 14 means discern.

"New wine" comes from a verbal root meaning to tread, or to press (v. 11). "Wine," a different word, is fermented, but "new wine" is not. Indulged in together, these beverages rob a man of the rational ability to orient himself. An example of Israel's confused thinking is her abandonment of normal means of revelation for Canaanite practices (v. 12). "My people" is covenant language. How could Israel, God's chosen people, turn from their heritage of revelation through the law and through direct encounter to seek direction from a block of wood? The word translated "inquire" (literally, "ask") is technical language for seeking counsel from oracles (Judg. 1:1). "A thing of wood" could be an idol of wood, the Asherah beside the altar in Canaanite shrines, or an oracle tree. "Staff" probably alludes to a Babylonian practice of divination by rods or wands. The procedure involved the holding of two sticks upright, murmuring incantations over them, and then letting them fall. The way the sticks fell would guide the inquirer.

The word rendered "spirit" in the phrase "spirit of harlotry" may be translated wind, or power (v. 12b). Israel had been overcome by a power that they were no longer able to control. It caused them to err. Their harlotry expressed their rebellious betrayal of God, Israel's true husband. Both men and women were committing adultery and playing the harlot in the worship of Baal, the Canaanite god of fertility (v. 13). God placed responsibility for the corruption of the women (v. 13b) at the feet of the men (v. 14b). Hosea closed the oracle with a warning based on a wisdom saying (v. 14c). No doubt "a people" refers to Israel. "Ruin" (thrust down) would be the result of their participation in Canaanite cultic practices.

God's Counsel to Judah (4:15-19)

Hosea warned Judah to avoid the sinful ways of Israel (v. 15). "Guilty" means deserving blame in regard to religious matters. Its exclusive use in the Book of Hosea is to describe the guilt Israel incurred by participation in the cult of Baal. For Judah to worship at Gilgal or Bethel would be to become "guilty" along with Israel. The warning to Judah was bitter condemnation of Israel's religious practices, whether Judeans were inclined to visit Israel's favorite shrines or not.

Gilgal had been a popular shrine in the Jordan Valley since Israel's first entry into the Land of Promise (Josh. 4:19). But Hosea followed Amos in his low evaluation of it (Hos. 9:15; 12:11; Amos 5:5). "Bethaven," house of iniquity, refers to "Bethel," house of god, a pun Hosea may have adapted from Amos (Amos 5:5). Hosea warned Judah against taking a religious oath at these shrines because they had become so tainted with Baalism. Israel's stubbornness served as a barrier to God's shepherding care of Israel (v. 16). "Ephraim" was so wed to idolatry that Hosea counseled Judah to "let him alone." Their drunkenness and harlotry had dragged them down to shame (v. 18). "Wind" (v. 19) is the same word that is translated "spirit" in verse 12. With the word, Hosea described the captivating force that pulled Israel down to ruin and shame.

God's Condemnation of Israel's Leaders (5:1-7)

Hosea indicted three groups of leaders in Israel for failure to provide justice: "priests," "house of Israel," and "house of the king." The "priests" are those already named in God's lawsuit against Israel (4:4). "House of Israel" refers to the representatives of the people, not simply to the people. "House of the king" designates the royal court. All of Israel's leaders are included.

Three imperative verbs reveal the urgency of Hosea's message to Israel's leaders. "Hear" implies heeding as well as attentive listening. "Give heed" means attend to, or sharpen the ears for attentive listening. "Hearken" means turn the ear to give close attention. Why should these leaders give such careful attention to the prophet's message? It is because the administration of justice is the unique function of these leaders.

God's charge against Israel's leaders is cast in hunting terminology. A "snare" is a trap for catching birds. A "net" may be used to catch birds (Hos. 7:12) or lions (Ezek. 19:8). A "pit" was dug in the earth and covered over so that the unwary prey would fall into it. Israel's leaders had become traps to rob the people of life and liberty instead of being their protectors and benefactors. Hosea may have selected sites where Israel's leaders had led her to worship false gods. Because of their failure God will "chastise" them.

Some of Israel's leaders may have objected to Hosea's message. "Know" contains the idea of intimate, firsthand, experiential knowledge. "I" is emphatic. It may refer to God, as it does in the previous verse, or it may point to the prophet as the one who knows Israel so well. Israel was an open book to both God and Hosea. "Played the harlot" means that Israel, God's wife, had become a harlot by participation in the cult of Baal (1:2; 4:4-14). Thus, Israel had become unclean (and thereby unfit for communion with God), like an adulterous woman (6:10).

"Their deeds" refers to the cultic activities associated with the worship of Baal (v. 4). "Permit" is literally "give." The word rendered "return" is the term usually used in the Old Testament to mean repentance. The paralyzing power of Israel's sin has barred her from returning to God. They are so much under the power of harlotry connected with Baal worship that they do not "know," or acknowledge Yahweh as their God. "Within them" means at the core of Israel's corporate life. God knows all about Israel, but Israel does not know God.

Israel's "pride" was her confidence in the effectiveness of the fertility cult (v. 5). They felt no need for God. The root meaning of the word translated "testifies" is answer. It is a legal term for introducing prejudicial evidence in a trial (1 Sam. 12:3; 2 Sam.

1:16). Israel's pride condemned her. Her "guilt," iniquity, or punishment for iniquity would cause Israel to "stumble" and fall.

Israel's fall would come through failure of their ceremonial worship (vv. 6-7). "Flocks" and "herds" suggest the response of a people whose guilt was overwhelming. So burdened with the sense of sin were they that they brought the whole herd to sacrifice to God, not just one animal selected from the herd. "Seek" is the technical word for seeking God through ritual acts at a sanctuary. But their extravagant offerings would be to no avail. Perhaps they forgot that "to obey is better than sacrifice" (1 Sam. 15:22). Hosea declares, "they will not find him" (v. 6). The reason their search would be futile is that God "has withdrawn from them." It is not that God cannot be found. Rather he will not be found through Israel's Baalized cult. God will not be manipulated by sacrifices, no matter how numerous.

The word translated "they have dealt faithlessly" denotes Israel's covenant-breaking activities expressed by their participation in the fertility cult (v. 7). The word rendered "alien" means not only foreigner but what is alien in contrast to what should have been an intimate relationship with God. The reference to "the new moon" eating up the people and the allotted portions of land suggests the Baalization of that festival. God's punishment for participation would be severe.

God's Promised Judgment upon Israel (5:8-15)

The setting for this oracle is the Syro-Ephraimitic War. Israel allied with Syria in response to the threat of Assyrian aggression in 735 BC. The pressure Tiglath-pileser III of Assyria put on this coalition caused them to seek support from Judah. They attacked Judah for refusal to join them. Ahaz, Judah's king, promptly appealed to Tiglath-pileser III for help. Assyria responded immediately. Then Judah launched a counterattack on Israel. Verses 8-12 contain an account of Judah's retaliation.

The sound of the "horn" signaled the approach of an invader (v. 8). The particular cities named suggest that Judah was the enemy coming against "Ephraim" (Israel) from the direction of Jerusalem. Gibeah (hill) was three miles north of Jerusalem; Ramah (elevated) was two miles beyond Gibeah; and Bethaven (a scornful name for Bethel) was six miles past Ramah on the road through Benjamin.

Judah's corrective action would leave Israel "a desolation," or waste (v. 9). The verb translated "I declare" is literally "I cause to know." "What is sure" is that which has been confirmed. The prophet was not thrashing around hoping to find the truth. He had it. Ephraim certainly would become a desolation.

Judah's retaliation against Israel is compared to the crime of removing a landmark (v. 10). Offenders could expect the curse of God (Deut. 27:17). His "wrath" (overflowing fury) would be poured out like water upon them. Already Ephraim had been crushed by Tiglath-pileser III (v. 11). The reason such judgment came was Israel's foolish coalition with Syria. God's judgment upon Israel and Judah is expressed in two bold metaphors. "Moth" and "dry rot" work slowly and unnoticed. Just so God is at work destroying both kingdoms.

At separate times Israel and Judah made the same mistake of seeking help from Assyria (v. 13). "The great king," Tiglath-pileser III, was not able to help either nation. The third metaphor Hosea used to picture God's actions against these sister kingdoms is that of a lion. With emphatic language, God is pictured as a fierce lion, bringing quick and total destruction to Israel and Judah (v. 14). "I, even I, will rend" is literally, "I, I, I will rend." "None shall rescue" means that Israel and Judah would be without hope.

The threats of judgment against Israel are followed by a word of mercy (v. 15). Earlier (5:6) the prophet warned Israel not to rely on extravagant rituals in their search for God. Now God threatens withdrawal, "return . . . to my place," but the word "until" leaves the door ajar. God can be found and his favor secured if Israel will admit her "guilt" and seek God's presence.

God's Desire for Israel (6:1-6)

Verses 1-3 contain a song of repentance. In times of national crisis such songs were sung by the people as they gathered for fasting, lament, prayer, and sacrifice. The song is linked in the Revised Standard Version translation to 5:15 by use of the word "saying." That word is in the Greek and Syriac versions, but it is missing from the Hebrew text. The song (6:1-3) may be God's counsel to repentant Israelites about appropriate words by which to seek him. Yet the words seem to reflect a shallow understanding of the tough demands of true repentance. God appears as an indulgent grandfather. He would revive the nation without the necessity of contrition.

The song may be Hosea's invitation to his fellow Israelites to repent. "Come" and "let us return" reflect the urgency of his appeal (v. 1). "Return" in Hosea's vocabulary means leave off the practices associated with the worship of Baal and go back to the relationship with God in the wilderness period. His appeal is based on the nature of God. The one who has "torn" is the one who will "heal." He alone can deliver, for he alone is God (Deut. 32:39).

"After two days . . . on the third day" (v. 2) likely refers to the period associated with covenant renewal in Israel (2 Sam. 20:4; Ezra 10:8-9). "Revive" means preserve alive. The urgency of knowing God is expressed in two imperatives "let us know," and, literally, "let us pursue to know" (v. 3). The certainty of God's "going forth" is illustrated by seasonal metaphors. The "dawn" comes every day with predictable regularity. In the same way, seasonal rains come to "water the earth." God is that reliable.

Israel's response was disappointing, if the song of repentance was Hosea's call to national renewal. Therefore another interpretation is offered. The song could be a liturgical piece composed by priests in response to Hosea's judgment oracle. The priests picked up typical Hosean words, such as "return" and "know." But they addressed Yahweh with the song as though he were a nature god.

The questions of verse 4 have the ring of an exasperated father. He has tried everything but failed to get the appropriate response from his incorrigible son. What dismayed God was the lack of constancy and permanence in Israel's covenant "love" (v. 4). It was as temporary as a "morning cloud" or "the dew that goes early away."

Israel's love had been so superficial and unreliable that God had resorted to radical treatment of Israel. "Therefore" (v. 5) suggests that the harsh treatment God gave Israel was based on their vaporous love (v. 4b). Through "prophets" like Elijah, Elisha, and Amos, God had tried to correct Israel (v. 5). His acts of judgment against Israel were not done in a corner. They went forth like the light so that all could see. Real return to God involves "steadfast love" and "the knowledge of God" (v. 6). These personal relationship words are set over against the acts of "sacrifice" and "burnt offerings." What God desires is faith and obedience, not a religion of rituals.

Israel's Disloyalty to the Covenant (6:7-11)

What God looked for in Israel was "steadfast love" and "the knowledge of God." What he found was covenant breaking and evil. Whether the phrase translated "at Adam" refers to a city, an Adamic covenant, or the proneness of Israel to break covenant is difficult to decide. Not the place names but what was happening at the places named seems to be the important thing. Gilead is described as a "city of evildoers" (v. 8). "Tracked with blood" suggests violent crimes. Robbery, murder, and villainy are the crimes associated with Shechem (v. 9). Even the "priests" became involved in the evils of the age.

Israel's "horrible thing" was harlotry (v. 10). The result of Israel's wholesale participation in the rites associated with the fertility cult was ritual defilement. To be "defiled" meant to be disqualified to approach God. The word to Judah (v. 11) serves as a warning that the tragedy of Israel has a prophetic meaning for them.

Love: The Fruit of Righteous Living
7:1 to 10:15

Nothing in chapters 7 through 10 indicates that Israel had been practicing righteousness. But in the midst of political assassinations, religious perversion, and social chaos, Hosea promised God's love for Israel (10:12). The nation could count on a bumper crop of God's loyal love any time they would sow the seeds of righteous living.

Israel's Fallen Kings (7:1-7)

The Revised Standard Version translation reveals the tie between 6:11b and 7:1a. "When I would restore the fortunes of my people" (6:11b) is parallel to "when I would heal Israel" (7:1a). Many times in the past God had "restored" and "healed" Israel. Once more Israel needed God's mercy.

The verb translated "heal" may mean forgive (14:5). Hosea uses this word alone to express forgiveness. Both heal and forgive seem to apply here. Israel sought other healers to no avail (5:13). Only the Lord could heal Israel's wounds, and his willingness to do so had not diminished. But a barrier stood in the way. When God would restore and heal Israel, her "corruption" and "wicked deeds" (iniquity) thwarted God's grace and forgiveness.

Probably "my people" (6:11b) and "Israel" (7:1a) are synonymous. Similarly, "Ephraim" (7:1b) and "Samaria" (7:1c) are parallel references. With the terms "Ephraim" and "Samaria," Hosea designated the Northern Kingdom of Israel.

The word translated "corruption" (7:1b) may mean iniquity or guilt. "Is revealed" is from a verbal root that means uncover or remove. The same word refers to the exposure of Hosea's wayward wife in 2:12. The point here is that Israel's iniquity is in full view.

"Wicked deeds" is from a plural noun in a relationship to "Samaria." The word pair relationship could be rendered "evils of Samaria." "Wicked deeds of Samaria" probably points to the capital city as the source of the nation's sin (compare Mic. 1:5). The verb "is revealed" (7:1b) applies to "the wicked deeds of Samaria" as well as "the corruption of Ephraim." Both stood stark naked before God's penetrating gaze.

The root idea in the verb translated "deal" is do, or make. This word usually implies hostility toward the Lord. Treachery and deception are associated with the word here in 7:1. "Falsely" may suggest sham repentance (6:1-3), or political treachery (5:11,13). The basic meaning of the term is to deceive. Israel's pious words were not matched by righteous living.

The noun translated "thief" (7:1) comes from a verb that means to steal. "Breaks in" is more forceful than the root idea in the term from which it is translated. The basic idea in the root is to come, to go, or to enter. A better rendering of the phrase would be "a thief enters." "The bandits" is from a verbal root that means penetrate or cut. The noun means inroad, or marauding band. "Raid" is the translation of a verb that means make a dash. "Consider" is literally "say to their heart." Not even in the confidence of their own hearts did they dare speak honestly. They knew the truth but refused to admit it even to themselves.

Attention is called to "all their evil works" (v. 2) by placement of the phrase in the emphatic position ahead of the verb. "Remember" means more than mental recall. It implies the recollection of what is past in order to make it current. For God to remember all of Israel's "evil works" is but a prelude to judging them for those works.

"Now" (7:2b) could be a designation of time, "at this very moment." It may mark a transition to the conclusion of verses 1-2a. Israel had become captive to her own evil deeds (compare 5:4). The term translated "before" means opposite or against. "Face" may mean me, my presence, or my favor. Thus, Israel's deeds may be opposed to God, visible to God, or a barrier to receiving God's favor. Perhaps all of these interpretations should be applied here.

Four of the last six kings who reigned in Israel were assassinated. These were Zechariah, Shallum, Pekahiah, and Pekah. Likely Pekah's assassination before Hoshea became king is the setting for 7:3-7. "They" in verses 3, 4, and 7 designates those responsible for the treacherous plots which resulted in the fall of "all their kings." Those charged with committing "evil works" (v. 2) must be the same ones who plotted the assassination of Israel's kings. Probably the reference is to Israel's political and religious leaders.

The word translated "their evil works" in verse 2 is rendered "their wickedness" in verse 3. "They make . . . glad" is an intensive verb and may be rendered "utterly make glad." The new king and his princes who were installed on the heels of the assassination of the previous king must be the ones made glad. The noun translated "treachery" is derived from a verb meaning be disappointing, deceive, fail, or grow lean. It is rendered "lying" frequently. The fact that it is a plural noun suggests repeated deception. One king after another came to the throne in Israel, not by God's appointment, but by wickedness (assassinations) and deception (lies).

Usually in the Book of Hosea, adultery means literal sexual unfaithfulness (3:1; 4:13-14). Here it stands for betrayal in worship. "They . . . all" refers to king, court, and conspirators. Those said to be unfaithful to the Lord in political matters are compared to a heated oven. The focus of the comparison is actually the fire in the oven. Unattended, such a fire would die down to smoldering ashes. While the baker kneaded the dough and waited for it to rise, he neglected the fire. In the same way the conspirators' political passions smoldered while their plot evolved.

Ovens of burnt clay were common in private dwellings. But mention of a "baker" suggests the royal court ovens in Samaria and professional bakers. Overnight the dough would rise and be ready the next morning to be cooked. The baker stirred the fire, added new fuel, made flat cakes and slapped them against the inner, curving walls to cook. Control of the fire of political passion until the right moment may be the intended analogy.

"The day of our king" (v. 5) probably means the coronation day of the candidate for king in whose behalf the plotters acted. Zimri used the "heat of wine" when he assassinated Elah (1 Kings 16:8-14). That may be the strategy used when Hoshea seized the throne from Pekah. At the scheduled time the conspirators got Pekah's princes drunk with wine, murdered Pekah, and installed Hoshea as king. The timing was coordinated with the Assyrian invasion (about 733 BC). "Heat of wine" may imply poisoned wine.

The last line of verse 5 reads literally, "his hand draws scorners." Is this a reference to the power of wine to attract the loudmouthed? Or, does the statement suggest that the king makes common cause with the conspirators? Perhaps the best interpretation is that the phrase describes physical assault, a violent attack with some kind of weapon.

Likely Hosea has continued here (v. 6) the description begun in verse 3 of the conspirators' rebellious plot. Their passions are like the fire in an oven. At night the fire "smolders," literally, sleeps. But in the morning with new wood the fire blazes again. From a plot which began in a secret conspiracy, the revolt broke out into the open with frenzied activity. Abruptly, the account breaks off without relating the actual assassination of the king.

Hosea used his "heated oven" metaphor once more as he closed the sorry story of Israel's political intrigue (v. 7). "All of them" seems to be a summary reference to that whole era of instability, characterized by the assassination of four of Israel's last six kings. Like ravenous beasts "they" devour their rulers. The verb translated "devour" is the regular term for eat. "Rulers" is from a noun whose verbal root means to judge.

"All their kings" is another summary reference to that period in Israel's history when one king after another fell at the hand of an assassin (v. 7b). The succession of kings had been by charismatic selection. No longer was that procedure followed in Israel. "None of them" refers either to the fallen kings or to the people of Israel. Not one of the kings had thought to cry out to God for deliverance from his assassin. No one from among the Israelites registered a protest to God, or looked to God for help. The kings and the people of Israel acted as if God had nothing to do with kingship.

Israel's Foolish Alliances (7:8-16)

With verse 8 the prophet shifted the subject from political revolt to foreign policy. "Mixes himself" is a technical term in cookery to designate a mixture of oil with flour. The simile implies that Israel was so mixed up with the "peoples" as to become one with them. God meant for them to be separate and different from the surrounding nations (Ex. 19:5-6). "Peoples" probably means surrounding nations with whom Israel had made alliances (v. 8). Word arrangement makes "Ephraim" emphatic. A literal translation reveals the author's emphasis: "Ephraim with the peoples he, even he, mixes himself."

The two culinary terms in verse 8 suggest continuity with the oven metaphor in verses 3-7. "A cake not turned" would be burned. The result would be a half-raw, half-burned, useless cake. The simile characterizes Israel's political folly. She turned to other nations for security and help. She needed to turn to God (v. 10). Refusal to do so would surely be disastrous for Israel.

The root meaning of the term translated "aliens" is stranger (v. 9). The verb form suggests that strangers had already devoured Israel's strength. Use of the verb "devour" may imply eating the produce of the soil. At least the word rendered "strength" often refers to agricultural products. "Strength" could simply refer to physical strength and virility. How could aliens eat up Israel's agricultural products, or sap her physical strength, and the nation not know it? The explanation may be that Ephraim was blinded by the temporary benefits of survival and security. An emphatic word order reveals Hosea's shock at Israel's ignorance of what was happening: "and he not he knows" (v. 9a, AT).

The term translated "gray hairs" is usually associated with old age. Again Hosea's shock is registered with the phrase, "and he knows it not." "Sprinkled" may be derived from an Arabic word meaning "to creep up to stealthily." The nation's corruption, weakness, and aging had been gradual and unnoticed.

Hosea 7:10a is identical in Hebrew to 5:5a, but Revised Standard Version translators rendered them differently. The primary difference is in the last word, translated "to his face" in 5:5a and "against him" in 7:10a. "In the faces of him" is a literal rendering of the term. It usually means "before him," or "in his presence." The verb rendered "witnesses" in 7:10a is translated "testifies" in 5:5a.

"Pride" is the translation of a noun derived from a verbal root meaning "rise up" (v. 10). The noun is translated "exaltation" frequently. Israel's pride manifested itself in a blind self-confidence and in a blatant move to make political alliances. That "pride" witnessed, or presented evidence, as in a court of law against Israel. Her own "pride" condemned her.

The verb rendered "return" is the usual word for repent in Hebrew (v. 10). "Seek" is a technical term to describe pilgrimage to a sanctuary to secure the favor of God. Blind pride kept Israel from turning to God for help and from seeking his favor. "This" points back to Israel's declining strength, signs of aging, and stubborn refusal to turn to God.

"Like a dove" is another simile Hosea used to describe Ephraim (v. 11). A fifth-century writer used the eighth-century prophet named Jonah (dove) to represent the narrow, exclusive attitude of Israel in that post-Exilic era. Here Israel is compared to a dove, and the dove traits are not complimentary to Israel. "Silly and without sense" is literally "simple and without heart." Perhaps Hosea had observed doves flitting here and there with no apparent goal or purpose. Israel's seesaw politics stemmed from her stupidity and instability.

"Egypt" and "Assyria" are in the emphatic position ahead of the verbs (v. 11). Not only so, but the expected prefixed prepositions on the two nouns are missing, making the language very terse. "Calling" and "going" describe the fluttering "dove" (Israel) in her senseless search for help. Foolishly Hoshea tried to switch loyalty from Assyria to Egypt. The form of the verbs implies that Israel had already sought help from these quarters.

God's response to Israel's frantic efforts to find help in political alliances is described in terms of a hunter trapping a bird (v. 12). A different form of the word "go" ("going" in v. 11) suggests an incompleted journey. God threatened to net the silly dove in her frantic flight for help. "Like birds of the air" is emphatic. The term translated "bring them down" is a form of a verb which means "go down." God's action would stop Israel's efforts to secure the help of the two major powers of the day. But God's ultimate purpose was chastisement. The Hebrew text has "according to the report to their congregation" instead of the Revised Standard Version translation "for their wicked deeds." What is at stake here is the basis of Israel's chastisement. Either the nation's "wicked deeds," or some "report" (perhaps of alliances made) would be the ground for God to chasten Israel.

"Woe to them" is an indirect threat (v. 13). It is parallel to "destruction to them" in the next line. The basis for the woe-saying was that Ephraim "rebelled" and "strayed" from God. The tone of these matching lines may be compassionate rather than vindictive. That interpretation is made probable by the final line in the verse: "I would redeem them, but they speak lies against me." Of course the Lord wanted to deliver Israel. He was willing and able to do so. The problem was not God's will, but Israel's waywardness.

The verb translated "redeem" was used in commercial law to describe the ransom or reclamation of a person or thing by payment. This word served to describe God's deliverance of Israel from Egyptian bondage (Ex. 15:13). But Israel's "lies" would prevent such an exodus from the Assyrian threat. Israel's contrary will and actions neutralized God's benevolent intentions.

Israel engaged in deceptive speech when they should have cried to God for help (v. 14). The verb translated "cry" is not the word for calling upon God in normal prayer times. It is the term for a cry of distress (Ex. 2:23). Their situation was desperate, but they did not respond with a sincere appeal for God's deliverance. "From the heart" means that Ephraim did not cry to God sincerely. A cry went up all right, but it was insincere.

Israel cried to God (8:2), but they dealt with him as though he were a Canaanite deity (7:14). "Wail" comes from a verbal root normally associated with the howling of an animal. To pronounce the word is to make a sound like a howl. Fertility rites connected with Baal worship involved adulterous "beds." Rituals of the Baal cult included gashing (1 Kings 18:28). The Revised Standard Version translators correctly followed the Septuagint which has the word for *cut* here (v. 14c). The preposition translated "for" is usually rendered over or upon. Over "grain and wine" the Israelites cut themselves in a ritual aimed at securing God's favor. Such cultic activity was common for Baal worshipers, but totally unacceptable for worshipers of God.

To employ Baal-like rituals in the worship of God was to "rebel" against God (v. 14d). "Rebel" is the translation of a verb that means turn aside. Israel turned aside from a simple and sincere "cry" to God and turned to a pagan ritual.

God alone had enabled Israel to cope with national crises in the past (v. 15). That fact is stated emphatically. "Trained" is from a verb that means correct or discipline. The verb translated "strengthened" means be or grow firm, strong, or strengthen. Both verbs are intensive in form. Each one needs a helping word to reflect its full force. "Utterly trained" and "utterly strengthened" reveal this feature of the original language. To say that God "strengthened their [Israel's] arms" is to designate him as the source of their power. Israel responded to God's provision with devious plots against God.

The verb translated "turn" is the term usually associated with repentance. But here Israel's turning is not to God, but to Baal and to the nations. Israel's comparison with a "treacherous bow" marks them as a people who have missed the target. "Their princes" is a reference to those who plotted assassinations and made foolish alliances. But an Egypt-like bondage would be "their derision." Their resistance to the prophetic word would surely provoke God's judgment. Death by the sword and bondage in a foreign land are the two aspects of God's judgment.

Israel's Full Punishment (8:1-14)

The trumpet blast and the circling vulture symbolize the full fury of God's judgment about to fall upon Israel (v. 1). That judgment would be military in nature and leave a trail of death. "Set the trumpet to your lips" is literally "unto your palate a horn." The absence of an expected imperative verb reflects the urgency of the summons. A ram's horn was used in military circles to signal the troops, or to alert a city that enemy troops approached.

The excitement evident in the summons to sound the alarm (v. 1a) clearly dominates the next phrase as well (v. 1b). It is a nominal sentence: "as the vulture over the house of the Lord." The verb "is" must be supplied. The "vulture" referred to was a large bird of prey, perhaps the griffon vulture, or eagle. Characteristics associated with the bird when used as a metaphor include swiftness, gluttony, and superiority. Reference is probably to a vulture-like enemy. "House of the Lord" is likely a reference to the land as God's gift to Israel (compare 9:8,15). Assyria may have been the "enemy" (v. 3), poised and ready to swoop down on the Lord's house. However, the simile is applied to God in many contexts.

On what basis would judgment come upon God's people? They broke his covenant, transgressed his law, and spurned the good (vv. 1-3). These were the root causes of the approaching disaster. The form of the verb rendered "broken" indicates completed action (v. 1). "Transgressed" fits the meaning here better than "broken." "My covenant" designates the formal agreement between God and Israel. God initiated the covenant, assumed responsibility for Israel's security, and established his lordship over them, but Israel had transgressed the covenant.

"My law" refers to the stipulations of the covenant between God and Israel. The term rendered "transgressed" means rebellion against known authority. A literal translation reveals that "against my law" is emphatic: "and against my law they have rebelled." Rebellion against God's "law" was rebellion against God.

The outrage of Israel's claim to know God is seen clearly against the backdrop of her covenant breaking and rebellion against God. The verb "know" implies an intimate relationship that simply did not exist. To address God as "My God" was to lay claim to a covenant relationship which in fact had been broken.

The third charge God made against Israel is found in verse 3: "Israel has spurned the good." A clear grasp of what is meant by "the good" is essential to an understanding of how serious this charge was. Everything that made life good under the covenant was included, and God was the source of "the good." That is what Israel "spurned." The form of the verb translated "has spurned" indicates completed action. "Rejected" may be a better word to convey the precise meaning of the verb here. It designates complete severance of relationships. To reject "the good" was to reject God. Pursuit by an unnamed enemy would be the disastrous consequence of rejecting "the good" (v. 3a). The form of the verb "pursue" implies an imminent attack not yet begun, or a current attack still in progress. "The enemy" is made emphatic by its placement before the verb. Who is "the enemy"? Yahweh? A foreign nation? One thing is certain: the enemy would be the agent to administer God's judgment upon Israel.

Two related evils in Israel served as evidence of her apostasy, making kings without consulting God and worshiping idols contrary to covenant norms (v. 4). God accused the people in general of making kings with no concern for God's choice and without his approval. "Not through me" suggests that God had nothing to do with it. With the inclusion of "princes," the whole government of Israel is denounced. "Without my knowledge" does not mean that God was oblivious to Israel's procedure. Rather, their choice of princes did not have God's approval.

Just why God connected king making and idol making is not altogether clear. Jeroboam I, Israel's first king, had set up calves at Bethel and Dan (1 Kings 12:28-29). That move was purely political and proved to be the source of sin for Israel, not only in Jeroboam's reign, but also throughout her whole history.

"Idols" is derived from a verb that means to shape or fashion (v. 4b). "Silver and gold" were examples of "the good" Israel received from God's hand. But God accused them of taking his "good" and making it into objects of pagan worship. The particular object meant may have been the "calf" referred to in verse 5. Both Israel's kings and her idols were man-made. God had no part in either one. The ultimate consequence of making idols with God's "good" silver and gold was "their own destruction." Israel should have known that all such objects were doomed to be destroyed.

Instead of rejecting "the good" from God's hand (v. 3), Israel should have rejected her "calf." God had rejected it (v. 5). Nothing aroused God's anger like idolatry. Jeroboam I may have thought of the calves set up at Bethel and Dan as pedestals or thrones for worship of the invisible God. But the people came ultimately to worship the idols themselves, as verse 6 reveals. Evidence is lacking that a calf ever stood in Samaria. Thus, the references to "your calf, O Samaria" and to "the calf of Samaria" must be examined carefully.

"Calf of Samaria" may be another way of referring to the royal sanctuary at Bethel. Amos called it "the king's sanctuary" and "a temple of the kingdom" (Amos 7:13). Hosea accused the inhabitants of Samaria of worshiping the calf at Bethel (10:5). Actually, Hosea used the disgraceful name "Bethaven" to designate Bethel. Amos coined this name when he declared that Bethel would "come to nought" (Amos 5:5). The word rendered "nought" is the term Hosea used to form the scornful nickname for Bethel. The "calf of Samaria" must have been the one at Bethel.

Hosea's typical word for divine wrath is used here to describe God's response to the calf of Samaria (8:5b). Israel's worship of foreign gods had always sparked God's burning anger (compare Ex.

32:10 ff.). The form of the verb translated "burns" reflects the full
accumulation of God's past reactions to Israel's idolatry. Now God's
wrath was fully developed. "Them" refers to all Israel as the object
of God's anger.

The words translated "how long" (v. 5c) are used regularly in
laments (Pss. 6:3; 13:1-2). "Pure" is used in laments to declare one's
innocence (Ps. 26:6). Here the cry of sorrow is over Israel's inability
to live free of guilt. The lament is over the fact that Israel's period of
impurity seems to have no end.

The words at the beginning of verse 6 have been joined in the
Revised Standard Version to the end of verse 5. "In Israel" is
literally "for from Israel." That phrase is followed in verse 6 by "and
he [that, it] an artisan he, even he made him [it] but not God [is] he
[it]" (AT). What is emphasized in the statement is that a mere man
made the object Israel venerated as God. Interpreters and translators may struggle for precision in handling the verse, but the utter
folly of worshiping a homemade god stands out as its major thrust.

The "calf of Samaria" could not offer the divine help Israel needed
(v. 6b). It was man-made and, therefore, not God. It was doomed to
destruction. The word translated "broken in pieces" implies that the
calf was carved of wood and covered with gold (8:4). It is a plural
noun meaning "splinters," and it is emphatic. Certainly no help
could be expected from a "calf" reduced to splinters.

Israel's foolish practice of depending on political alliances and
pagan gods was sure to bring God's judgment upon her (v. 7). The
agricultural metaphors in verse 7 reveal the connection between
Israel's present actions and the future consequences. "Wind" in
wisdom sayings stands for vanity, emptiness, nothingness (Prov.
11:29; Job 7:7). Israel's worship of the calf and trust in political
alliances would prove to be vain. The vanity of it all was not that
such sowing produced no harvest. Rather, it was that, true to the
laws of sowing and reaping, Israel would reap in kind and with
accelerating quantity. The "wind" of idol worship would produce a
"whirlwind" of disaster.

Rhyme, a rare feature in Hebrew poetry, characterizes the second
saying in verse 7. The terms rendered "heads" and "meal" are the
rhyming words. "Sprout" or "branch" is the usual translation of the
first word. The second word is derived from a verb that means "to
grind." Without growth for the standing grain, there would be
nothing to grind into flour. No growth, no grinding seems to be the

disappointing connection between the rhyming words. The concluding threat is that should the grain produce a harvest strangers
would eat it rather than Israel. God's people could take no comfort
in the prospect of a harvest in which they would not share.

"Devour" (v. 7) and "swallowed" (v. 8) come from the same verbal
root. Not only would aliens swallow Israel's grain harvest, should
there be one, but also Israel as a nation was already swallowed up.
The reference may be to the Assyrian invasion of Galilee and Gilead
in 733 BC when these regions became Assyrian provinces. Israel
was left a broken, "useless vessel." "Already they are among the
nations" (8:8) means that Israel had lost her distinctiveness (7:8) as
God's special treasure. All that remained for the nation was to be
discarded like a useless pot.

Use of the independent pronoun "they" in verses 9 and 13 ties
this block of material together as a unit. Ephraim's going up to
Assyria (v. 9) is related to their return to Egypt (v. 13). "They" is
emphatic in both verses. "They, even they, went up to Assyria" and
just as surely "they, even they, would return to Egypt" (AT). Why
did they go to Assyria? Both the metaphor of a "wild ass" and the
verb translated "wandering" suggest independent, willful action.
Ephraim is pictured as a friendless, forlorn figure. Hoshea sought
political security under Assyria's umbrella.

Part of the comparison of "Ephraim" to a "wild ass" involves a play
on words. Each term has the same consonants. The difference is in
the order of arrangement. "Wild ass" may suggest promiscuity,
rather than willful stubbornness. Both the verb rendered "has
hired" and the noun translated "lovers" bear out this line of
interpretation.

The threat of judgment upon Ephraim is based on their habit of
hiring allies among the nations (v. 10). The form of the verb
translated "hire" in verse 9 suggests completed action in the past.
Here in verse 10 the form implies incompleted action going on
currently. Because Ephraim persisted in hiring allies among the
nations, God vowed to "gather them up." His purpose in gathering
Israel must be for judgment.

The Revised Standard Version translators followed the Septuagint
in the last part of verse 10, "And they shall cease for a little while
from anointing king and princes." Doubtless the translators opted
for the Septuagint version because it seems to fit the context. The
judgment threatened is that soon Israel would be without any

government officials. They shut out God's participation in the choice of their kings. Now God would shut them out of having a king of any kind. That would be God's judgment upon Israel for seeking security in political alliances.

Israel's false worship is the focus of the Lord's accusation and threatened judgment in verses 11-13. The charge is similar to the earlier indictment against the priests (4:7). More priests meant more sin against God. Similarly, more altars meant more sinning (v. 11). Ephraim "multiplied" altars to deal with sin. But that only provided more places to commit sin.

Israel directed her attention to her many altars and lost sight of God's multitude of "laws" (v. 12). Their altars were familiar. God's laws were strange. Fervent participation in religious exercises was no substitute for faithful adherence to God's laws. How odd that God's covenant principles should be regarded as "a strange thing" by those who were parties to the covenant!

Sacrifice should express the worshipers' love for and trust in God. But the people of Israel offered sacrifices because they enjoyed the festivities related to the sacrificial system (v. 13). They must have thought that mere engagement in a ritual automatically established solidarity with God. Hosea's assessment of the end result of sacrifice was shattering. They delighted in sacrifice, but God did not delight in them. He did not accept them favorably.

"Now" introduces the verdict based on Israel's perverted religious exercises (v. 13*b*). In verse 12, reference to God is in first person, but in verse 13, the writer shifted to third person. Verse 12 is God's charge against Israel. Verse 13 is Hosea's evaluation of Israel and his announcement of God's judgment upon them. "He" designates God as the one who will remember Israel's iniquity. To "remember" suggests calling to mind in order to call to account. "Iniquity" generally designates moral crookedness, and "sin" suggests missing the mark. The verb rendered "punish" has the basic meaning of visit in order to determine guilt or innocence. Punishment might follow that assessment.

"Return to Egypt" would be Israel's specific punishment. A literal translation reflects the emphatic nature of the final phrase in verse 13: "they Egypt they shall return." Read verses 9:3 and 11:5 to clarify what "return to Egypt" means. Use of the phrase in parallel with the threat of Assyria suggests an option open to Israel, either to submit to Assyrian deportation or to flee to Egypt as refugees. Some interpreters take "return to Egypt" to be a reference to an Egypt-like bondage. Such a punishment would represent a complete reversal of Israel's salvation history.

Hosea accused Israel of forgetting God (2:13; 13:6), God's laws (4:6), and their Maker (8:14). Often "forget"means failure to show concern for. Perhaps the reader should note the contrast between Israel's forgetting their Maker and God's remembering their iniquities. Israel "built palaces" (or temples) to compensate for the fact that he had forgotten his Maker. It is not that Israel did not recall that God was the source of the nation's being. Rather, it was that the nation came to the place where no one cared that God gave them existence. They filled the vacuum created by failure to care with the tangible activity of a building program. Hosea had charged Israel with multiplying altars.

Now he accused Judah of multiplying fortified cities. Whereas Israel trusted in sacrifice for her security, Judah trusted in military preparedness. The Lord's response to Judah's frantic efforts to secure the nation from the threat of her enemies was an announcement of destruction. "Fire" was used as a strategy in warfare and came to symbolize war. Notice that God is the author of the "fire." With it he threatened to "devour" Israel's strongholds. Both Israel and Judah would feel the full fury of God's wrath upon them because of their forsaken faith.

Israel's Final Overthrow (9:1-17)

Israel's apostasy would end ultimately in their complete overthrow as a nation (9:17). Hosea's words of accusation and threat to that effect disrupted some jubilant festival. A likely choice is the Feast of Booths, an autumn harvest festival. Doubtless the setting was some worship site, possibly Bethel, Gilgal, or Samaria. The date for this material must have been the period immediately following the Syro-Ephraimitic war (about 733 BC).

Hosea's shattering words indicate that mourning would have been more appropriate for Israel than rejoicing (v. 1). The negative particle translated "not" is an immediate prohibition. "Do not now rejoice" is a precise rendering of the phrase. "Exult not" represents a slight textual change. The Hebrew text has, "Do not rejoice O Israel unto exultation like the peoples." Often the term "peoples" refers to God's people. Here the reference seems to be pagans.

Israel had sunk to the level of the surrounding nations in her worship.

Hosea accused Israel of harlotry (v. 1*b*). This is the basis for his prohibition against Israel's rejoicing. For Israel to attribute the bountiful harvest to Baal, the god of fertility, was to "play the harlot." To worship God as though he were Baal would amount to the same thing. The phrase "forsaking your God" is literally "from upon your God."

"Harlot's hire" refers to the fees received from the harlot's lovers (v. 1*c*). The term comes from a verbal root that means to give. Here the gifts represented by the word include grapes, fruit, and grain. Israel's "love" for these items was a perverse and lustful thing. The parallel nature of the two verbs, "played the harlot" and "loved," suggests love for making love as their motive rather than love for the fee. "All threshing floors" designates the location of Israel's perverted lust. Mention of the threshing floors may argue for actual participation in the rites associated with Baal worship. However, the reference may only suggest that the nation dealt with God as though he were Baal.

The disaster Hosea announced could not have been a crop failure (v. 2). At a harvest festival, the crop was already in. The prediction is that Israel would not enjoy it. They would not be fed (or shepherded) by "threshing floor" and "winevat." They would be disappointed by the "new wine." What the prophet implied was that the bounty Israel gathered to celebrate would become booty for an invading enemy (v. 3). The term translated "winevat" refers to a basin carved out of solid rock with a connecting deeper pit to collect the oil of olives or the juice of grapes. Grain, olive oil, and wine in abundance would normally bring joy to those gathered to celebrate God's gift of a bountiful harvest. But Hosea prohibited Israel from rejoicing. These products usually bringing satisfaction would disappoint and fail Israel. Verse 3 is Hosea's explanation of why that would be so.

The first reason the bountiful harvest would not feed and fulfill Israel's expectations is that the people would not be there to enjoy it (v. 3). Hosea declared that "they" (Israel) would not "remain in the land of the Lord." The verb rendered "remain" is usually translated "dwell." Israel would no longer live as settled and secure inhabitants of the land God gave them. Instead, they would "return to Egypt."

Israel's options were to return to the Lord and dwell securely in "the land of the Lord," or return to Egypt and "eat unclean food" in a foreign land. Observe that Assyria is parallel to Egypt. Many Israelites had already been deported to Assyria. The prophet expected others to flee to Egypt as refugees. Israel's salvation history would come to an end, and she would return to her pre-Exodus bondage. "Unclean food," in Hosea's view, was food prepared in a land ruled by a foreign god.

Israel's removal to an unclean land would bring their erring worship to an end. No longer could they pour libations of wine to Yahweh (v. 4). Their sacrifices would cease, and God's pleasure in their sacrifices would be no more. Their unclean food would make them ritually unclean and, therefore, unfit to approach God in worship. The "mourners' bread" was bread eaten by those in mourning for the dead. Contact with the dead made them unclean and, consequently, unfit for worship. Similarly, bread eaten in exile made deported Israelites unclean. The only legitimate use of such bread was "for their hunger" (life, survival).

Probably "the day of appointed festival" (v. 5) is a reference to Tabernacles, the autumn harvest festival. That celebration may be the one called "feast of the Lord" in Judges 21:19 and in the next line here in verse 5. The question of what Israel would do when the season to celebrate the festival came around is left unanswered. As deportees in Assyria or refugees in Egypt, they could not celebrate Tabernacles. All of their festivals would come to an end.

The Revised Standard Version translators emended the text of verse 6 to read "Assyria" without any textual evidence. It is certainly not required in the context as a parallel to "Egypt." "Memphis" serves that purpose. As the Hebrew text stands, it reads literally, "For behold they are going from destruction." "Going from destruction" probably means fleeing from the threat of an Assyrian attack. But escape to Egypt would be a gathering for death, not life. What Israel could expect to get from Egypt was burial, not salvation from her enemies. The very shrine where Israel's throngs gathered to celebrate would no longer be used. The site would be overgrown with "nettles" and "thorns."

The only insight in the entire Book of Hosea to the peoples' response to the prophet's preaching is found here in Hosea 9:7-9. It is a brief passage with no accompanying narrative to explain what was happening. Most interpreters conclude that the prophet quoted his opponents' slanderous words (v. 7b) and recorded their ugly deeds and attitudes (v. 8b).

Intensity of thought is achieved by the prophet's use of short, repetitious statements (v. 7a). Verb form for the term translated "have come" in both lines suggests completed action, but the context seems to call for either present or future tense. Present tense would result in the placement of emphasis upon the immediacy of the "punishment" and "recompense" referred to. Future tense would emphasize the certainty of the announced judgment from the speaker's point of view. The prophet's use of "days" (plural) instead of day suggests a period or season of punishment rather than one climactic and final moment. "Punishment" is derived from a verbal root meaning visit. Visitation for the purpose of determining guilt or innocence is its usual meaning. "Recompense" is essentially synonymous with "punishment." It means requital, or retribution. "Israel shall know it" means that Israel will experience in a personal and intimate way the announced judgment. Instead of joyful days of festival, Israel should prepare for awful days of judgment.

The scornful words in verse 7b must represent the peoples' response to the prophet's message. Doubtless the "prophet" is Hosea. Words chosen by the people to describe the prophet are aimed at discrediting him. The matching words are "fool" and "mad," meaning stupid (blockhead, or foolish talker) and crazy (enthusiastic babbling of a madman) respectively. "Prophet" and "man of the spirit" are the titles used by Hosea's opponents as they declared their rejection of the man and his message. The verbal root from which "prophet" comes means to bubble over (as in ecstatic speech), to announce, or to be called. "Man of the spirit" may be synonymous with the more popular "man of God," since the prophet was said to be overcome by the Spirit.

Hosea accused his opponents of responding to him and his message with scornful words because their great guilt generated great hostility (v. 7c). The words translated "your great iniquity" could be rendered "your great guilt." "Great hatred" comes from words that could properly be translated "great hostility." Total opposition is expressed by the term rendered "hatred."

Hosea identified his role as that of "watchman" of Ephraim (v. 8). By the term "watchman" the prophet pictured a person whose duty it was to watch from a tower to spot an approaching enemy. Either he was a watchman with God, or a watchman of Ephraim, "the people of my God." The thanks offered Hosea for his faithful watch was a trap set on every road and "hatred" (hostility) expressed by the whole populace. "The house of his God" probably refers to the land of Israel, not a shrine.

The prophet compared the peoples' response to him and his message with "the days of Gibeah" (v. 9). Is the point of comparison Israel's stubborn determination to have a king when Saul was chosen? Saul came from Gibeah (1 Sam. 8—15). Or is the reference to the shameful episode at Gibeah recorded in Judges 19—21? The latter reference is more likely. Israel's destructive deeds almost wiped out the tribe of Benjamin in that episode. The nation's current response to Hosea was ruinous just like their previous response had been. Hosea warned his opponents that God himself would "remember their iniquity" and "punish their sins." "Remember" means bring to current accountability. "Punish" means visit to assess guilt or innocence and then administer appropriate judgment.

Threat of national extinction for Israel ties Hosea 9:10-17 together as a unit. Differences in style and focus between this unit and the previous material in the book reveal a sharp break. Was Hosea forced to discontinue his public ministry for a time? That seems likely. Up to this point only passing references have been made to Israel's history. Now historical notices begin to dominate the text. The prophet traced Israel's present infidelity to their first encounter with and fall to Baal worship.

God's words about his initial meeting with Israel portray the Chosen People as an unexpected and delightful discovery (v. 10). To find "grapes in the wilderness" would be surprising, since grapevines do not usually grow there. The "first fruit on the fig tree" was especially delectable. Both analogies reveal God's delight in Israel in his initial encounter with them. Hosea usually locates the beginning of God's relationship to Israel in Egypt (2:15; 11:1; 12:9,13; 13:4). But the choice here of "the wilderness" as the place where God "found" Israel puts God's election adjacent to Israel's apostasy at Baal-peor. That seems to be the reason for selecting the wilderness as the scene of Israel's election.

As Hosea's wife betrayed him, so Israel betrayed God when she came into contact with the Canaanite cult of Baal (v. 10b). "Baal-peor" may denote a locality, rather than a god by that name. However, the two terms as they are arranged may be translated

"Baal of Peor." Hosea's reference must be to Israel's illicit relations with Moabite women at Shittim (Num. 25). The women of Moab invited Israel to their sacrifices (Num. 25:2), and as a result "Israel yoked himself to Baal of Peor" (Num. 25:3). Hosea's description of what Israel did at "Baal-peor" (v. 10b) is parallel to this statement in Numbers 25:3. "Consecrated themselves to Baal" and "yoked himself to Baal of Peor" seem to refer to the same event. One aspect of the verb translated "consecrated" is related to oath-taking. Nazirite comes from this verbal root. The noun rendered "Baal" is literally "shame," but the Revised Standard Version translators correctly understood the word to be a designation for Baal. For people to become what they love is a repeated principle in Scripture. Israel loved Baal and, like the object of their love, became "detestable."

God's judgment upon "Ephraim" is cast in a form similar to a fertility curse. Their involvement in fertility rites associated with the cult of Baal would not produce offspring as they hoped. Ephraim's "glory" centered in the presence and blessings of her covenant God. But that "glory" was about to "fly away like a bird." The form of the verb translated "fly away" suggests flight under its own power. That fact implies that departure of God's glory is the subject under discussion. From a different perspective, the birth of numerous children was looked upon as Israel's chief glory. Contextual evidence (vv. 11-14) lends support to this position. Total barrenness is pictured in verse 11. But due consideration must be given to God's explicit warning in verse 12: "Woe to them when I [God] depart from them." God's departure and Israel's barrenness were two sides of the same coin.

The judgment announced in verse 11 is total barrenness. Possible exceptions are held up for consideration in verse 12. But God warns parents who may succeed in bringing up children that he will personally "bereave them till none is left." The grammatical structure of the word translated "till none is left" is identical to the series of words rendered "no birth, no pregnancy, no conception." A literal translation, "no man," reveals the parallel construction. Here the threat of a total removal of the population is associated with God's warning of his departure.

Verses 13 and 14 are Hosea's words to Ephraim. Like hunter's game, Ephraim's sons had been exposed to the danger of pursuit and slaughter. Hosea must have witnessed Israel's troops being slaughtered by Tiglath-pileser's superior forces during the Syro-Ephraimitic War. The only prospect the prophet held out for the future was wholesale slaughter (v. 13b).

The framework for the prophet's prayer (v. 14) is what he had already witnessed of Israel's slaughter and what he expected to see in the future (v. 13). He seems to be torn between obedience to God in his role as a prophet and compassion for his people as one of the sons of their fathers. Already he had announced that Ephraim would be scattered (v. 11a), their mothers would be barren (v. 11b), their children would die (vv. 12a, 13), and their God would abandon them (v. 12b). As he began to pray for his God-forsaken people he was at a loss to phrase an appropriate petition in their behalf. What blessing from God could he request? His choice for a blessing was one of the words of punishment. What ordinarily would be looked upon as a curse would be a blessing in the terrible days ahead. For mothers to be barren would be better than witnessing the slaughter of their children. The participle translated "miscarrying" (v. 14b) is from the same verbal root as the term rendered "I will bereave them" (v. 12).

The dialogue between God and Hosea extends through verses 15 and 16. Yahweh rejected the prophet's intercession and repeated the threat of barrenness, slaughter, and rejection. The prophet tied the current failure of kingship with its historical antecedent in Gilgal. The beginnings of the monarchy under Saul and his rejection are associated with Gilgal (1 Sam. 11:15; 15:12,21). Both political (1 Sam. 11:15; 15:12,21) and religious failure (Hos. 4:15; 12:11) are connected with Gilgal. "Hate" (becoming an enemy) describes God's response to Israel's commitment of "evil" there. To tie "every evil" of Israel to Gilgal reflects just how serious God considered the root cause of Israel's current political and religious failures. "Wickedness" comes from the same root as "evil." Based on the wickedness of Israel's deeds, God threatened to "drive them out" of his house. "Out of my house" means "from my domain," not "out of my shrine." Such a radical response from God implied cancellation of the covenant.

"Love" in verse 15c is not from the term for covenant love. It is from the word that frequently means initiating, or election love (11:1). "Not will I cause to add love to them" is a literal translation of the phrase rendered "I will love them no more." The phrase seems to mean that once God drives Israel from his domain he will never initiate love for them again. The reason given is that "all their princes are rebels." These "princes" were responsible for leading the people. But their stubborn, rebellious spirit ("rebels") made them blind guides leading the blind.

The form of the verb translated "is stricken" (v. 16) suggests that Ephraim had been smitten in the past and remained in that condition. The same can be said for Ephraim's barrenness, referred to under the figure of a dried-up root. It had been dried-up, and it remained dried-up. As a direct consequence, "fruit" would not be produced by Israel. Verse 16b is practically a duplicate of verses 12a and 13b. The slayer of 13b seems to be some foreign invader. Here in verse 16 God is the one who will "slay" (literally "cause to die") their children.

Hosea is the spokesman in verse 17. Now he agrees with God's verdict: "My God will cast them off." The essential idea in the verb rendered "will cast them off" is reject. Why should God reject Ephraim? Because they have not obeyed God. Ephraim's punishment will be to become "wanderers among the nations." They would be homeless as well as childless. Israel's final overthrow is pictured in pitiful terms of a childless, homeless people who have lost their identity.

Israel's Fallow Ground (10:1-15)

Hosea presented the possibility of a new beginning for Israel (10:12). But the nation would have to meet certain conditions for that possibility to become a reality. They had to sow the seeds of righteous living if they wanted to reap God's loyal love. God's refreshing rain of salvation would follow Israel's earnest search for God.

Israel's religious life is the primary theme of verses 1-8. Twice Hosea injected the subject of kingship into the discussion (vv. 3 and 7) and then proceeded to announce God's devastating judgment upon both Israel's religion and king. Israel's history is not a rags to riches, but a success to failure story. God had poured out his blessings upon his people, but they had consistently misused his gifts. Hosea pictured Israel as "a luxuriant vine," producing a bountiful yield. As a vine planted, cultivated, and blessed by God, Israel would naturally produce much "fruit."

With increased fruit Israel multiplied her altars (v. 1b). As good came to the land they embellished their "pillars." Israel had adapted Canaanite "pillars" to their worship and had used them as memorials. But now their use had the full implication of Canaanite fertility rites. The multiplication of altars and the beautification of pillars made Israel blameworthy because their hearts were "false" (v. 2).

A "false" heart (v. 2) caused Israel to multiply altars and embellish pillars in an effort to ensure God's continued blessing. Their religious activities did not represent wholehearted devotion to God. The verb translated "is false" means divided. Israel approached the altars and pillars with one eye upon the ritual with a pretended devotion to God and the other eye upon the bountiful yield they hoped to obtain. Their divided heart made them guilty and deserving of God's punishment. Israel would not draw near to God in true devotion at the altars, but God would draw near to them in judgment as he came to destroy the altars. "The Lord" would be the one who would "break down" Israel's altars and "destroy" his pillars. Without the altars and pillars, Israel could no longer pretend to seek God through a ritual aimed at materialistic ends.

Verse 3 is connected with verse 2 as a second result of Israel's divided heart. Their sanctuaries would be destroyed (v. 2), and their king would be spurned (v. 3). Both parts of this verdict would be realized in the future. Yahweh had been rejected as king when the people pressed Samuel to give them a king like the surrounding nations. Now the prophet envisioned a time when Israel would acknowledge that in truth they had "no king." The cause of Israel's kingless condition was their lack of reverence ("fear") for Yahweh. Their own kingmaking without any reference to God had proved to be futile (8:4). In the future Israel would confess the complete ineffectiveness of kings set up without reverence for God or reference to God. The expected answer to the rhetorical question "and a king, what could he do for us?" is "Nothing!"

Israel's past experience with their kings formed a good summary of what they could expect from future kings (v. 4b). "They utter mere words" probably means "they make promises," but they do not follow through with fulfilling deeds. "Empty oaths" likely refers to the oaths taken by the king to work for the best interests of the people. The "covenants" were the treaties made between the king and the people. "Judgment" was the duty of Israel's kings. They were responsible for maintaining order and safety for all the citizens. But the kind of king who "utters mere words," takes "empty oaths," and makes meaningless "covenants" will dispense justice that kills "like poisonous weeds."

Hosea shifted the subject from kingmaking in verses 3 and 4 to calf worship in verses 5 and 6. The feminine plural "heifers" is rendered "calf" (v. 5) by the Revised Standard Version translators, bringing it into accord with the masculine singular "calf" in Hosea 8:5-6. However, this plural form may designate the female counterpart to the "calf of Samaria" (8:6). Again Hosea employed "Beth-aven," his scornful name for Bethel. "Inhabitants of Samaria" designates the permanent residents of the capital city. They were stirred up over the crisis caused by Assyria (v. 6). What they feared was that their central object of worship, representing the power and the presence of their god, was in danger of being lost.

"Its people" and "its idolatrous priests" are both related to the endangered object of worship (v. 5b). Devotees and worship leaders gathered to engage in services of mourning for their threatened god. God's people of the covenant had become Baal's people. Hosea called the clergy associated with Bethel (house of God) pagan priests. Already the costly decorations of the object of worship had been used to pay the heavy tribute exacted by the Assyrians. Its "glory" had departed. The ultimate shame that remained was for the object of worship "itself" to be carried to Assyria (v. 6). "Tribute" suggests that the calf image would be "carried" as tribute, not taken as spoil. Even the verb rendered "carried" is used regularly to denote the giving of gifts, or the payment of tribute. Ephraim would have to accept (literally, "take") shame because they worshiped a powerless "idol."

No evidence is available to support the designation of any king of Israel as "Samaria's king" (v. 7). This fact has led some interpreters to the conclusion that the words refer to the "idol" mentioned in verse 6. But in a context (10:1-8) dealing with the failure of both Israel's worship and kingship, it seems better to handle verse 7 as a concluding remark about the king. That is followed in verse 8 with a similar concluding remark about Israel's worship. Both Israel's kingship and worship will come to an end.

The word translated "the high places" is used ordinarily to designate places of pagan worship (v. 8). "Aven" means wickedness. Earlier the worship site at Bethel (house of God) was tabbed house of wickedness (Bethaven, v. 5). Now the prophet announced that all the high places in Israel would be "destroyed" because they too were places of wickedness (Aven). These places epitomized "the sin of Israel." The growth of "thorn and thistle" on Israel's altars indicates their complete abandonment and disuse. In utter dismay, Israel's inhabitants will cry out to the mountains, "Cover us," and to the hills, "Fall on us." This is a plea, in the face of the threatening circumstances described in verses 7 and 8, either to be hidden or to die.

Already Hosea had traced Israel's sin back to Baal-peor and Gilgal. He had also added Gibeah to the list of places where her sin had its origin (9:9). In verse 9 Hosea picked up this line of argument again.

The verb translated "you have sinned" (v. 9) is the term that means "to miss the mark." Word order makes "from the days of Gibeah" emphatic. Israel's sin was no new development. It had been going on a long time. "There they have continued" is literally "there they have stood." The verb means "to persist in the same attitude," or "to remain unchanged." Israel's stubborn persistence in Gibeah-like sin will bring down an appropriate Gibeah-like judgment of "war."

"I will come" (v. 10) is taken from the Septuagint. The Hebrew text has "in my desire." It is the Lord himself who will "chastise" Israel. That chastisement will be administered by "nations . . . gathered" against them. Israel was due such divine discipline because of her "double iniquity." What is meant by "double iniquity"? Is it two idols, or the present Gibeah-like sin and its historical antecedent, or spiritual adultery and political plotting?

God's election of Ephraim is described with agricultural metaphors (v. 11 ff.). "A trained heifer" was one that was broken in, submissive to the farmer. That's how Ephraim was in the early days when first chosen by God. "Loved to thresh" suggests service in which the nation delighted.

Ephraim's election was for service. "Her fair neck" qualified her for "yoke" service in Canaan (v. 11). God expected the harder work of plowing and harrowing from his Chosen People. "Ephraim," "Judah," and "Jacob" seem to designate the same people here, even though in other places the names have distinct meanings. The mixture of covenant terms with agricultural language (v. 12) shows that God intended for Israel to perform the harder task of becoming his convenant people. Plowing would prepare the soil for the seed.

Harrowing would cultivate the growing plant. But Israel must "sow" the seed of "righteousness" to "reap" the fruit of covenant "love." The nation must "break up" the "fallow ground" of her neglected opportunity. They must "seek the Lord" in true devotion before they could expect him to appear with the gift of "salvation."

What Israel actually did was altogether different from what God expected (v. 13). They had "plowed" all right. But they had planted the seed of "iniquity" (wickedness). Appropriately "injustice" (wrong) is what they had reaped. Instead of enjoying the "rain" of salvation, they had "eaten the fruit of lies."

Israel's trust in military strength led logically to war (v. 13b-14). They trusted their way rather than God's way. The Septuagint has "in your chariots," but the Hebrew text has "in your way." God's way was not to trust in "the multitude of . . . warriors." But "the tumult of war" would arise in Israel as a test of her trust in military strength. Amid battle cries and falling fortresses, Israel's people and king would perish.

The judgment upon Israel is compared to Shalman's destruction of Beth-arbel (v. 14b), an event which must have been well known to Hosea's audience. But no other evidence than this verse is available to help identify Shalman or the destruction. Some interpreters take "Shalman" to be a reference to Shalmaneser V who succeeded Tiglath-pileser as king of Assyria. A more likely proposal is that it refers to Salamanu of Moab. Tiglath-pileser named him as one who paid him tribute. Cruel slaughter of women and children characterized the destruction of Beth-arbel.

"Thus it shall be done to you" (v. 15) points back to the Beth-arbel reference in verse 14. Instead of "Israel" the Hebrew text has "Bethel," a good parallel to "Beth-arbel." Israel's "great wickedness" was trust in her military prowess instead of trust in God. Israel's king, who incarnated their independence from God, would be the first to fall. "In the storm" is literally "at the dawn" referring to the beginning of battle. "Utterly cut off" means destroy. The king of Israel would surely be destroyed. Israel had no hope of experiencing God's love as long as her covenant obligations remained unattended like fallow ground.

Love: The Hope of New Life
11:1 to 14:9

Again in chapter 11 Hosea turned to Israel's history to explain current conditions in the nation. Love was God's motive when he elected Israel by delivering them from Egyptian bondage. From the beginning Israel flaunted that love. Stubborn apostasy dominated their response then and that spirit characterized the nation in Hosea's day. But God's strong love formed the basis of Israel's hope for new life in the future (14:4-7).

God's Love for Israel (11:1-12)

The intense love of God for Israel dominates chapters 11—14. Israel's apostasy seemed to require God's complete rejection and national extermination. But God's love had prevented such a tragedy from the beginning. The present crisis was no exception.

The portrayal of Yahweh as father and Israel as his son is unmatched in the entire Old Testament for tenderness of relationship between God and his people. Israel was but a "child" when God's electing love moved him to call his "son" from Egypt. With the term translated "child" Israel is pictured as a youthful, dependent people when God initiated his relationship to them. Hosea was the first to employ "love" as the basis of Yahweh's relationship to Israel. "Called" is covenant terminology (compare Jer. 31:32). It implies the formation of a relationship. Here it means that Israel was adopted as God's "son." Like a father Yahweh loved, trained, and provided for his son Israel.

"The more I called them" is from the Septuagint (v. 2). "They called to them" in the Hebrew text may be correct. If so the reference is to the "Baals" and "idols" in the next two lines. "The more they went from me" is based on the Septuagint. The Hebrew text has "thus they went from them." Whether the Baals and idols called and Israel responded positively, or God called and Israel rebelled against that call, the end result was the same. God's election call (v. 1) was soon followed by his correction call (v. 2). "They went from me" is a picture of rebellion. "They shall go after the Lord" makes use of the same verb to predict restoration (v. 10).

Two parallel statements show the way Israel displayed the prodigal attitude toward Yahweh (v. 2b). Word order makes "to the Baals" and "to idols" emphatic. "Sacrificing to the Baals" was rebellion against God. "Burning incense to idols" is practically parallel to the previous statement. Both phrases describe Israel's apostasy.

How could "Ephraim" rebel against the one who taught him to walk, healed his hurts, and provided his needs? Emphatic language is used to stress the fact that God himself served Israel in the role of a father (vv. 3-4). A literal translation reveals the emphasis: "But I, even I, taught Ephraim to walk." The verb translated "taught . . . to walk" has the root meaning of "to foot it." The form used here may mean "train to walk." What a tender scene! The proud father holds the hands of his young son as he takes his first faltering steps.

Israel's failure to appreciate Yahweh's tender care is expressed in terms of ignorance. "Know" is a covenant word to express formal acknowledgement of the second party to a covenant (v. 3b). In general usage, it expresses intimate and personal experience. What is it that Israel did not know? "Healed" may mean either physical recovery, or spiritual forgiveness. God may be lamenting the fact that Israel did not know that he truly forgave them, even after they fell into idolatry.

A major question for interpreters of verse 4 is whether or not there is a change of metaphor from child (vv. 1-3) to work animal. The subject of verse 4 seems to be the benevolent actions of God toward Israel, an extension of the list begun in verse 3. Two parallel phrases in verse 4a make the message plain, though the metaphor is not so clear. "With cords of compassion" and "with the bands of love" describe how God related to Israel as a covenant partner. The same two words for rope are used in Isaiah 5:18 to describe a false covenant. Here in verse 4 they signify a true covenant. And it is a covenant based on God's love. The verb rendered "led" has as its root meaning "to draw," or "to drag." In Jeremiah 31:3 this word is linked with "love" in a context of covenant-making.

The last two statements in verse 4 portray God as Israel's liberator, "one who eases the yoke on their jaws," and provider, "I bent down to them and fed them." Some interpreters insist that the metaphor of father and child is maintained here. If so Yahweh is depicted as a gentle father and an adequate provider. Frequently the verb translated "I bent down" is used in contexts where response to prayer is the subject. In such a case, the word is translated "incline." If that is its use here, then feeding Israel was God's response to prayer.

Return to Egypt may be symbolic of an Egypt-like bondage, toward which Israel was moving (v. 5). Already Assyria was their real ruler. Hoshea was only a vassal, subject to the Assyrians. Because Israel refused to "return" to God, they would "return" to Egypt. But this time they would be in bondage to the Assyrians.

Israel's stubborn refusal to return to God would result in the judgment of war and destruction (v. 6). "Sword" is the symbol of war since it was the primary weapon in warfare. The verb translated "rage" means "swirl," "twist," "turn." It affords a graphic description of a soldier's use of a sword in combat. "Against their cities" suggests the general destruction expected from the predicted war. "Gates" of cities were secured by "bars." With bars consumed by war, the gates could no longer be secured and the citizens would be exposed to the destruction of the invader. The verb rendered "consume" has several shades of meaning. It may mean complete, at an end, finished, accomplished, or spent. Here the word seems to mean "finish off." Reference is to the "bars" of the gates.

"Sword" is the subject of the three verbs in verse 6. It is the "sword" that will "rage," "consume," and "devour." "Fortresses" may be correct, but the Hebrew text has "counsels." Israel's proneness to follow her own plans sealed her doom. The nation sought security in allegiance to Baal and in alliances with other nations. The "sword" was God's judgment upon these acts of rebellion.

"My people" is covenant terminology. How absurd that God's covenant partners should be "bent on turning away" from him! The verb rendered "bent" usually means "hang." Israel's hang-up, or addiction, was backsliding. Again and again, they turned away from God. "Yoke" is used often in the Old Testament as a symbol of subjection. No power on earth could raise Israel's yoke of bondage.

God has stated his accusation against Israel in the language of court litigation (vv. 1-7). They deserved complete abandonment and full punishment. But God loved Israel. What could he do? Here in verse 8 the prophet pictures God in a painful conflict. Both justice and logic demanded that God abandon his stubborn, idolatrous son. But because of his love and because he is God and not man, he could not "give . . . up" his child. The verb rendered "can I give you up" means complete surrender. The matching line has a similar verb. It means deliver up to an adversary.

Israel would become like Admah and Zeboiim if God exposed them to the full fury of his wrath (v. 8b). "Make" is from the same verb used in the first line of verse 8 and translated "give" there. "Treat" comes from a verb that means set, place, or put. Its use here suggests the idea of putting Israel in the position for complete destruction. Admah and Zeboiim were destroyed along with Sodom and Gomorrah in the time of Abraham (Gen. 19; Deut. 29:23). These cities existed only as a memory of sudden and complete destruction. How could God do that to his son whom he loved? His heart recoiled from such a tragic course of action (v. 8c). "Recoils" comes from a verb that means turn or change. "Heart" designates the center of a person's will and mind. A change of heart here is very close to the word for repentance in the New Testament. "My compassion grows warm and tender" is literally "together they burn, my compassions." The idea in the verbal root from which "compassion" comes is "be sorry," "moved to pity," or "have compassion." Divine wrath is tempered by divine love.

The Lord's change of heart is indicated in verse 9 by use of the strongest negative in Hebrew in two matching lines. A literal translation of those lines reveals the parallelism: "Not will I do my burning anger,/Not will I return to destroy Ephraim." Justification for God's new course of action is simply that he is "God and not man." "Holy One" is from a word that means separate and distinct. "In your midst" suggests that God is accessible and available. Because he is God he will not "destroy" his people.

The turn in the heart of God would effect the return of Israel to God (v. 10). With emphatic phrases, the prophet described Israel's return to the homeland. A literal translation shows Hosea's emphases: "After Yahweh they will walk, like a lion he will roar; for he, even he, will roar and they will tremble, sons from the sea (west)." For Israel to walk after Yahweh is in contrast to their former walk away from him. Here a new exodus for Israel is in prospect. But they must respond to the lion's roar of God's voice and come trembling behind him as he leads them back home.

Israel's "trembling" (v. 11) implies fear lest they offend God. "Trembling like birds" suggests that in the nation's second exodus the people would be subdued and timid. A bad connotation is attached to Hosea's earlier use of "dove" as a metaphor for Israel

(7:11). Their going to Egypt and Assyria was to develop alliances with them. Their return with trembling would be the result of God's guidance with a view toward settling them in their homes. The verb translated "I will return them" should be rendered "I will cause them to settle."

Verse 12 fits the context of chapter 12 better than the message of 11:1-11. Actually verse 12 is verse 1 of chapter 12 in the Hebrew text. "Ephraim" comes out on the short end when compared to "Judah." "Lies" and "deceit" may both signify idol worship. "Known" and "faithful" are positive covenant words. The first two characterize Ephraim and the second two portray Judah.

Israel's Rebellion Against God (12:1-14)

Israel's deception and betrayal of God dominate chapter 12. For Israel to make alliances with foreign powers and then try to cover up the practice with "falsehood" and "violence" was foolish (v. 1). The nation's covenant-making activities with foreign governments were acts of infidelity to Yahweh. Parallel lines picture Ephraim foolishly herding the wind and pursuing the east wind (v. 1a). "Herds" and "pursues" are participles indicating continued activity. How silly to chase the wind all day long and day after day! It is futile because it is impossible to succeed. The "wind" is too illusive and the "east wind" is too powerful and destructive. King Hoshea's vassal-treaty with Assyria was the "east wind" (2 Kings 17:3) and his efforts to get Egypt to help in breaking it was the "wind" (2 Kings 17:4). "Make a bargain" is literally "cut a covenant." The "oil" carried to Egypt ratified the agreement Hoshea negotiated with the Egyptian ruler.

The form of the prophetic saying that begins in verse 2 is very similar to the form used in 4:1. There the defendant is "Israel." Here the defendant is "Judah." Both contain the term used to announce a legal suit. Both concern the breach of their covenant with God. The covenant infringements in chapter 4 are centered in Israel's social and civil life. Here in chapter 12 the scope is international.

The word translated "indictment" here in verse 2 was rendered "controversy" in 4:1. God is the plaintiff in both cases, while Israel is the defendant in 4:1 and Judah is the defendant here. Some interpreters believe that Israel was named originally in this indictment, and at a later time Judah was inserted to apply the oracle to

the Southern Kingdom. Use of "Jacob" in the parallel line that
follows would seem to rule that Judah and Jacob are synonymous—
though in the larger context "Jacob" may designate the old Israel
before the division of the kingdom. The trickery of the common
ancestor is used to explain the treachery of his contemporary
offspring.

"According to his ways" points to the basis for assessing Jacob's
guilt (v. 2). "Ways" means life-style, or bent in life. "Deeds" is
parallel to "ways," except that it usually refers to the bad practices of
a person, while "ways" is a more neutral term. "Requite" is from a
form of the verb that means turn or return. The principle is that bad
practices have a way of returning in the form of punishment upon
the practicer.

The historical references to Jacob, the ancestor of the contemporary nation, demonstrate consistent deception (vv. 3-4). What he
was before birth he continued into maturity. What he was as a
person he passed on to the nation. Hosea's Israel was a chip off the
old block. The name of "Jacob" is concealed in the verb translated
"he took . . . by the heel." In the same way "Israel" is hidden in the
verb rendered "strove." First, Jacob supplanted Esau then he
sought to overpower God. Jacob refused to let go of Esau and the
person at Penuel (Gen. 32:22-32).

The person with whom Jacob "strove" is called "the angel" in
verse 4. Both the language in Genesis 32 and Jacob's naming the
place Peniel (face of God) seem to confirm that the person was God,
or the angel representing God. If Jacob "wept" as he sought the
favor of the person at Penuel, the Genesis account has no reference
to it. The root idea in the verb rendered "prevailed" is "able."
"Grace" is the basic meaning of the verb translated "sought . . .
favor."

"Bethel" is emphatic (v. 4c). That's where Jacob "met" God. The
verb translated "met" is usually rendered "find." Literally the text
reads, "Bethel, he found him." The implication in the context is that
Jacob found God there, but the word for "God" is not in the text.
Neither is it used in the next line where the Revised Standard
Version has "and there God spoke with him." But the context here
and in Genesis makes clear that God is the one who spoke to Jacob.

A doxological announcement of the sacred name of God (v. 5) calls
the reader to a reverent hearing of God's message in verse 6.
Literally translated, verse 5 reads: "and Yahweh the God of the

hosts, Yahweh is his name (memorial)." "God of hosts" identifies Yahweh as the God of absolute power. Verse 6 appears to be a report of what God said to Jacob at Bethel. But in Hosea, this is an appeal for Israel to return to her God. Jacob did indeed return from a foreign land with the help of his God. But Israel needs to return from foreign alliances and foreign gods. Only God's help could make Israel's return possible. "You" is emphatic. A literal rendering of the line makes Hosea's emphasis clear: "And you, by your God, you return."

The verb translated "hold fast" means keep (v. 6*b*). What Israel was to keep was "love" and "justice," basic covenant requirements. Only here does Hosea exhort Israel to "wait" anxiously for God. "Wait continually" is in contrast to the nation's flighty nature (6:4). Israel's return to God would be possible with God's help. But the nation must be marked by "love," "justice," and constant waiting for God.

"A trader" (v. 7) is the translation of the term that is usually rendered Canaan. It designates the Canaanite spirit of harlotry and commerce in Israel. Deceitful traders used "false balances" to cheat unsuspecting customers. Israel loved to oppress because such activities lined their pockets with unlawful gain.

Hosea quoted Israel in order to present proof of guilt in the defendant's own words (v. 8). "I am rich" is from a verb form that suggests completed action. "Rich" was not a station Israel hoped to reach, but one already attained. The matching idea in the next line is literally, "I have found manly vigor (wealth) for me." "Wealth" is from the word rendered "strove" in verse 3. Ephraim was a self-made man, made wealthy by deceit.

A play on words is obvious in verse 8. The positive statement is that Ephraim had found wealth. The negative statement, using the same verb, is that they would not be found guilty. Use of the same verb and similarity of sound for the words translated "wealth" and "guilt" are the evidences of word play. Ephraim's claim was that in no way could "guilt" be found in the way he had found "wealth." Such a statement is a blatant rejection of covenant regulations.

God answered Ephraim's self-assertion, "I am rich," with the self-introduction, "I am [Yahweh]" (v. 9). The plaintiff making accusations in the earlier verses has become the judge announcing punishment in this verse. His right to judge is based on who he is.

"Yahweh" is Israel's covenant God. "Your God" implies that Yahweh is not some Baal who is concerned to give them riches, but their God to whom they are accountable for how they get riches. "From the land of Egypt" identifies Yahweh as their deliverer and the creator of their relationship as his people.

Their punishment will be to become tent-dwellers again (v. 9b). "As in the days of the appointed feast" is a reference to the Feast of Tabernacles. During the festival, Israelites dwelt in temporary booths set up for the days of celebration. But more than ritual reenactment of desert dwelling is implied. Those who refused to repent and return to Yahweh would be returned to the wilderness situation. Their alternatives were to dwell in their "homes" by returning to God (11:11) or to dwell in "tents" if they refused to return. What Israel performed as a temporary ritual would become a harsh reality again.

God's method of guiding Israel through the ministry of prophets (v. 10) began with Moses (v. 13). Through "visions" and "parables" God revealed his will to the prophets. They in turn mediated the divine message to God's people. "I spoke" suggests words endued with power to set in motion the judgment announced.

Gilead is described in Hosea 6:8 as "a city of evildoers." The term translated "iniquity" here (12:11) is the first part of the word rendered "evildoers" in 6:8. That Gilead would "come to nought" is the announced judgment upon that evil city (v. 11a). They would experience the futility of their own deceit. Hosea calls religious perversion evil (4:15; 10:8; 5:8; 9:5). That is probably the import of the term in this Gilead reference.

The "sacrifice" of bulls was not wrong (v. 11b). But in Gilgal the cult was pagan and the offerings were presented to Canaanite gods. For the altars of Gilgal to become "like stone heaps" would be for that site to suffer the same fate as Gilead. Their altars would have no more meaning than "stone heaps" piled up by farmers as they cleared their fields for cultivation.

The contents of verses 12 and 13 form a study in contrasts. Jacob, Israel's ancestor, is contrasted with Yahweh, Israel's God. Jacob fled for his life to the land of Aram, but God caused Israel to come to life out of the land of bondage. Jacob served (in lieu of the bride-price) for a wife, but the Lord served (a gracious, liberating act) by a prophet. Jacob kept sheep, but the Lord kept Israel. Both "herded" and "preserved" come from the same word. That word is normally translated "keep."

Verse 12 contains another historical reference to Jacob. His trickery in securing the birthright and the blessing from Esau may be contained in the mention of his flight to Aram. Moses must be the "prophet" referred to in verse 13. Israel's identity needed to be associated with God's redemptive act (v. 13), not the Jacob tradition (v. 12).

Hosea's Israel had looked to the trickster Jacob for a model and had vexed Yahweh bitterly (v. 14). The verb translated "has given . . . provocation" is used regularly for the provocation of Yahweh by worship of other gods. The Lord's punishment for this offense is announced in verse 14b. "Bloodguilt" designates a murderer. "Leave" may mean forsake, let alone, or abandon. It is a picture of a guilty, God-forsaken man. "Reproaches" are the taunts cast at Israel's God because of Israel's participation in pagan cults. But the punishment for Israel will be that their Lord (master) will cause these reproaches to fall back upon Israel.

Israel's Death as a Nation (13:1-16)

The setting for chapter 13 seems to be just before 724 BC when Shalmaneser V began the siege of Samaria. Hoshea had already been imprisoned by the Assyrians (v. 10), and Hosea had been driven to the southern border of Israel, near Bethel or Gilgal (12:4,11). Ephraim's power and influence were pervading. So superior was he that his words struck terror in his hearers (v. 1). If "Ephraim" designates the region where the royal residence of Samaria was located, the statement that "men trembled" when he spoke is very understandable. Many political decisions from that quarter in the past twenty years had brought terror to both Israel and Judah.

Between Ephraim's previous prominence and Israel's present, pitiful condition, something radical intervened. That something was his "guilt through Baal" (v. 1b). The verb rendered "incurred guilt" means to commit an offense, or to become guilty. Their offense was involvement with Baal. The result was that the nation "died." Verb choice suggests that their death was already an accomplished fact.

The word "now" implies that contemporary Israel is addressed in verse 2. "They sin more and more" is literally "they cause to add to sin." What "Ephraim" had done in the past to incur "guilt through Baal" the nation had continued to do to the present and in accelerating degree. The term translated "molten images" (v. 2) is used to refer to the golden calf in Exodus 32. Israel's law forbade the general use of images in worship (Ex. 20:4; 34:17; Lev. 19:4). "The work of craftsmen" is not a compliment to those who made the idols. Rather, it shows the absurdity of worshiping a man-made object.

The Revised Standard Version translation follows the Septuagint, not the Hebrew text in verse 2c. Thus, the question of human sacrifices is avoided. But the horror of human sacrifice seems to be the reference in the Hebrew text. The cultic kissing of the idol of Baal is attested in 1 Kings 19:18. Human sacrifice and veneration of a man-made calf idol reveal Israel's complete inversion of values. The sacrifice of "calves" was a normal part of Yahweh worship, but here the calves receive homage. Humans are sacrificed to a metal casting of a calf. How absurd!

"Therefore" (v. 3) introduces God's judgment upon Ephraim based on the indictment in verses 1 and 2. Simply put, the indictment is idolatry, and the verdict is impermanence. "They shall be" implies a direct connection between the object of worship and the character of the worshiper. Idols are nothing, and those who worship idols become nothing. Hosea's four similes say, as by one voice, "Ephraim has no future." "Morning mist" does not last long. "Dew" dries up early in the day. "Chaff" is dispersed quickly by the wind. "Smoke" exits through a window and fades into the air. All of these things disappear quickly and leave no trace. Such will be the judgment upon Ephraim, quick and complete.

The self-identification formula in verse 4 is identical to the one found in 12:9. In 12:9 it was used to establish the basis of God's judgment. Here it is used as the basis for Yahweh's exclusive role as Israel's God. The form of the verb translated "know" suggests that Israel had never known any other God but Yahweh. "Your God from the land of Egypt" means that Israel came to know God through the Exodus experience. "Know" is an election word related to God's covenant with Israel. God's claim to be Israel's only savior condemns Israel's habit of seeking saviors from other quarters. The nation looked for deliverance from their king, from military power, from political alliances, and from idols. None of them proved to be saviors.

Sometimes the verb translated "know" describes marriage, the most intimate of human relations (2:14-20). That seems to be its meaning in verse 5. With emphatic language, God declared that he came to know Israel. "In the wilderness" designates the historic moment when that happened. "The land of drought" reminds the reader of a prominent feature of the wilderness. "Knew" (v. 5) may mean the recognition extended by a suzerain (a conquering king) to a vassal (a conquered people). The Septuagint has "I shepherded you" instead of "I . . . knew you." Whether as husband, suzerain, or shepherd, God met the needs of his dependent people. And it was God's saving acts in Egypt and in the wilderness that made Israel's response (v. 6) so deserving of punishment and God's judgment (vv. 7-8) so fierce.

Filled with **the** bounty of God's provision (v. 6), they lifted up their hearts in pride and "forgot" God. In figures fierce and frightening, God pronounced judgment upon ungrateful Israel (vv. 7-8). The metaphors used to express the fury of God's wrath cast him as the enemy of the flock. God said he would be to Israel like a lion, a leopard, and a bear. The shepherd would become the enemy of the herd. A roaming lion, a lurking leopard, and a raging bear all picture a quality in God's judgment that is aimed at more than inflicting a wound. The attack would end in death.

In direct address, God declared his determined purpose to "destroy" Israel (v. 9). Hosea used the same idea earlier to express the nation's self-destruction (9:9) and to describe Yahweh's judgment (11:9). The verb form here implies finished and irrevocable destruction. The only helper Israel had was God, and now he had become their destroyer. No one could rescue the nation.

The questions in verse 10 imply either that Hoshea had already been imprisoned by Shalmaneser V or that Israel's king was helpless before the developing Assyrian siege. Israel had expected salvation from her kings and princes from the beginning of the monarchy. Kingship was their idea, not God's (1 Sam. 8:4-9). Their clamor for a king was a rejection of God as their king.

God's answer to the nation's request for a king was but an expression of his anger (v. 11). He gave them a king all right, but it was a left-handed gift. All the people could expect from it was the wrath of God. Whether Saul the first king or more recent kings are in view, God's gift in "anger" and taking away in "wrath" fit the circumstances of one and all.

Much as legal documents were preserved in a safe place for later reference, so Ephraim's "iniquity" (rejection of God as their king) was "bound up" for judgment in the future (v. 12). In Isaiah 8:16 "bind up" is related to the preservation of prophetic teachings. Here reference is to the retention of guilt. The general terms "iniquity" and "sin" cover the nation's apostasy to Baal, idolatry, and trust in kings. Israel's "sin" is "kept in store" like some treasure hidden for later use.

Israel's plight is compared to that of an unborn child stubbornly resisting the time for birth and subsequent life (v. 13). The mother's labor pains signal the time for the child to emerge from the womb. Ephraim's time had come for birth, for new life, and he did not recognize it. The punishment the nation had suffered thus far had been aimed at eliciting a return to Yahweh and new life. But like an "unwise son" that will not be born, Ephraim can only have death as his future. "Present himself" is literally "stand." With the negative it pictures the nation's stubborn refusal to respond positively to God.

Verse 14 may be interpreted as an announcement of salvation or as an oracle of judgment. As a message of redemption it makes no difference whether the verse contains questions or assertions. Either Yahweh is questioning whether or not to respond with redemptive actions or he is announcing them. "Compassion is hid from my eyes" would mean that God had decided against a course of vengeance. This interpretation would require the translation "vengeance" instead of "compassion" in the last line. It is "vengeance" that is hid from God's eyes. Paul applied this word from Hosea to his discussion of resurrection as a positive note of salvation (1 Cor. 15:55).

In the context, verse 14 could well be a message of radical judgment. The nation's sin (v. 12) and stubbornness (v. 13) seem to demand it. The language of verse 14a may be handled as questions. God was their only helper. He alone had power over Sheol and death. He was their sole savior. He could do it. But would he do it? The answer of the last line seems to be, No! The nation was in a death grip from which God would not rescue them.

Both "ransom" and "redeem" denote benevolent acts to benefit helpless persons (v. 14a). The first suggests liberation from legal debt by payment of a price. The second implies the duty of a kinsman to protect the rights of a relative. "Death" is the condition of a person whose life has departed. "Sheol" is the residence of all such persons. The questions of ransom and redemption imply that the nation had lost its life already and had begun to reside in Sheol. "Plagues" cause death and "Sheol" causes "destruction." The questions in verse 14*b* represent a call to "death" and "Sheol" to perform their ruinous work. God may exercise "compassion" in another time and place, but not now.

Ephraim may flourish for a time, or at least seem to be fruitful (v. 15). But the east wind of God's judgment would put an end to his fruitfulness. The "east wind" is identified as the "wind of the Lord." The term translated "wind" in the latter phrase is rendered "spirit" or "power" in other contexts. Here "the east wind, the wind of the Lord" must be a metaphor for Assyria. That conclusion seems assured by the switch in the last line of verse 15 to the language of military conquest. To strip the treasury of a conquered nation was a common practice of conquering kings.

Samaria, the capital city, would receive the brunt of God's judgment upon the nation (v. 16). "Shall bear her guilt" means that the city deserved the punishment about to be announced. Rebellion against her God was justification enough for the harsh judgment of destruction by a vicious enemy. "By the sword" designates the weapon by which the masses would die. Hideous methods were used in border warfare to kill the "little ones," along with mothers and their unborn infants. Not only would that decimate the population, but also it would discourage retaliation. The meaning of this three-part judgment announcement is all too clear. Death is the penalty upon God's obstinate son.

Israel's Hope for New Life (14:1-9)

The final message in the Book of Hosea (14:1-9) is a word of hope to balance the oracle of judgment in chapter 13. This balance is characteristic of Hosea (chs. 1—3). Catch words repeated from chapter 11 alert the reader to the relationship between the message there and the final salvation oracle here. Most of the words in chapter 14 can be found in the previous chapters. This fact makes chapter 14 a positive summary and conclusions section. The prophet's call to repent (vv. 1-2*a*) is matched by a proposed prayer of penitence as the way to return to God (vv. 2*b*-3). Only after Israel met the demand for repentance would God bestow his promised salvation (vv. 4-8).

The urgency of the exhortation to repent is expressed with an imperative form of the verb "return" (v. 1). In direct address, the prophet called on the entire apostate nation to return to Yahweh. They had turned from God to follow Baal. Now they must backtrack along the same path. Use of singular verbs and pronouns implies that the prophet thought of the people as one entity. Their need for repentance was based on the fact that already they had "stumbled" in their "iniquity."

The offering appropriate to Israel's return to God is "words" (v. 2). "Take," "return," and "say" are imperatives. Repentant Israel is ordered to take "words," not animals, as they make their way back to God. Words may be spoken from the teeth out and bear no true message from the person who speaks them. But words may become the vehicles for conveying heartfelt meaning. Inner changes and commitments need to be verbalized to become real (Rom. 10:9-10). It was from the Lord that Israel had turned to idols. It must be "to the Lord" that they return. Most sinners need more than an urgent appeal to repent. They need to be told how to do it and with what words to come.

A good evangelist helps the penitent sinner phrase words appropriate to repentance (v. 2b). "All" is placed first in the sentence for emphasis. Not just outwardly obvious sins, but all sins need to be lifted up and carried away. Israel had stumbled because of "iniquity" and, thus, it was iniquity that needed to be taken away. The verb translated "take away" means lift up and bear away. That's what the scapegoat did symbolically on the Day of Atonement. Here the prayer is to be addressed to Yahweh, for he is the only one who can remove Israel's sins. The petition for God to take away "all iniquity" is a confession of sin on Israel's part. At the same time, it expresses faith in God to forgive and remove the guilt of sin.

"Good" is a versatile word (v. 2b). Israel is said to have "spurned the good" in a context where "good" is practically equivalent to God (8:3). In another setting, hope is expressed that one day Israel would "come in fear to the Lord and to his goodness" (3:5). Again "Lord" and "goodness" are matched. "Goodness" in 3:5 may refer to the good gifts of God. But here in chapter 14 "good" is what Israel asks God to take as a token of repentance and commitment. What is penitent Israel's "good"? Apparently it is the "words" with which the nation returns to God.

The verb translated "we will render" means "requite," or "make good" (v. 2c). "The fruit of our lips" is what Israel pledged to make good. If God would take their words as an offering, they promised to live by them as a guide.

Verse 2 contains Israel's confession of sin in general, "Take away all iniquity." Verse 3 focuses upon the specific sins of the nation. "Assyria shall not save us" (v. 3a) is Israel's way of saying, "No longer will we trust in foreign alliances." "We will not ride upon horses" (v. 3b) means that Israel would no longer rely on military prepared- ness for security.

Never again would Israel say "Our God" to man-made idols (v. 3c). For Israel to renounce all false saviors was for her to place herself wholly in the hands of Yahweh. "In thee" is emphatic (v. 3d). In God alone would the orphan Israel find mercy. A noun built on the verb translated "mercy" means womb. The verb expresses the kind of intimate compassion shared by twins from the same womb. This kind of mercy Israel expected to find in God.

How God would respond to repentant Israel is expressed in verses 4-8. Israel's basic sickness was turning away from God to false saviors (11:5,7). "Faithfulness" is, literally, "turning" (v. 4a), the word used in 11:7. That is what God, the physician, promised to cure. "Heal" is part of Hosea's salvation vocabulary (5:13; 6:1; 7:1). The term suggests return to wholeness. In some contexts it means forgive. They have confessed turning from God; God promises to forgive their turnings. Forgiving and healing are two parts of the one cure.

"I will love them freely" is God's second salvation promise to Israel (v. 4b). Israel's wickedness had elicited God's terrifying pledge, "I will love them no more" (9:15). But now Israel's repentance would produce God's promise, "I will love them freely." God's love would be the source of healing and the power of life for Israel. The verb for "love" here is not the loyal love required to maintain the covenant. It is initiating love designed to begin a relationship. The term translated "freely" may be rendered "willingly," or "spontaneously." The meaning is that God's love is not based on merit. Israel's return to God would be met by God's healing and loving them. God's "anger" had resulted in Israel's fall (8:5; 13:11). No longer would he relate to Israel in anger (v. 4c). Now God's love would dominate his relationship to Israel.

God's third salvation promise to the repentant nation is that he would "be as the dew to Israel" (v. 5). Dew in a dry climate is especially refreshing and invigorating. God's relationship to Israel as "dew" would produce beauty, security, growth, protection, and fruitfulness in them. Use of language descriptive of flourishing plant life is a common practice in wisdom literature to express love between a man and a woman (Song of Sol.). Here such images are used to describe God's love for Israel.

"Blossom" (vv. 5,7) suggests beauty. "Strike root" (v. 5) implies stability. "Spread out" (literally "walk") describes growth and expansion. "Beauty" and "fragrance" picture the quality of pleasantness. "They" refers to Israel, and "my" refers to God. The imagery is clearly concerned with God's people becoming productive, not a plantation producing crops. Israel would "return" to God to settle under the protection of his shadow. In that relationship Israel would "flourish as a garden." She would become the precious "vine" God intended her to be (10:1; Isa. 5:1 ff.). God would give Israel new life.

"Ephraim" is Hosea's name for the contemporary Northern Kingdom (v. 8). God's question calls upon the nation to put an end to their involvement with "idols." Death, not life, was the issue of Ephraim's trust in idols. But God's promise to Israel is abundant life. Implicit in the description of God's bountiful provision for Israel is a contrasting unfavorable provision by the idols (v. 8b,c). In emphatic language, God declared that he (not the Baals) answered and looked after Israel. "Answer" implies God's favorable response to Israel's petitions. "Look after" suggests watching over to protect. In a final metaphor (used only here in the Old Testament), God asserted that he would be like a tree to Israel. The productivity and vitality Ephraim sought in Baalism was to be found only in God. "From me comes your fruit" is literally "from me your fruit is found."

The concluding verse (v. 9) is cast in wisdom language. It is a summary of the entire book: The righteous find good footing in walking God's paths, but transgressors stumble in them. It is an appeal for the reader to listen, learn, and benefit from the message of the prophet. Only the "wise" and "discerning" ones may "understand" deeply and "know" intimately the message of Hosea. What is that message? It is that the Lord's ways are right (straight, the norm), and righteous ones walk in them and find life.

JOEL

Introduction

Of crucial value in hearing the message of Joel in our time is the accurate placement of his prophecies in his time. The reader needs to know who Joel was, where he ministered, and when his message was first heard.

The Prophet

Joel's interest in sacrifice and his references to priests have caused some interpreters to conclude that he was among the priests. That conclusion seems unlikely. His prophecies are introduced with the exact language used to present the messages of prophets such as Hosea, Micah, and Zephaniah. His statements about priests and sacrifices suggest a perspective outside the priesthood. He is represented in the role of a prophet, not a priest.

The prophet's popular name means Yahweh is God. His father was named Pethuel (or Bethuel, in the Septuagint). Joel possessed excellent literary skills.

Joel may have lived in Jerusalem. The description of the locust attack on that city reads like an eyewitness account. He seemed to have firsthand acquaintance with sacrificial rites and priestly activities which were carried on there. His geographical references indicate personal knowledge of Judah, especially of the city of Jerusalem and nearby areas.

The Prophecies

Joel witnessed a devastating locust attack upon Judah and interpreted it as a judgment from God and as a symbol of the day of the Lord. He urged the people of God to repent and to expect God to save them and to bless them. The nations would be judged and Judah would be preserved as the dwelling place of God's people.

The canonical position of Joel's prophecies between Hosea and

Amos has led some interpreters to place Joel among the earliest of the classical prophets. The Books of Hosea, Amos, Micah, Zephaniah, Haggai, and Zechariah contain notations of reigning kings in the times of the respective prophets. Joel has no such notation. Book arrangement in the Septuagint may offer some help in fixing the date of Joel's prophecies. In that old Greek version Hosea, Amos, and Micah are grouped together, presumably, because their superscriptions date them according to the reigns of eighth-century kings. But Joel is positioned among the undated Books of Obadiah and Jonah. The Hebrew arrangement of Joel between Hosea and Amos must have been based on a literary link between Joel and Amos (Joel 4:16,18 and Amos 1:2; 9:13). The arranger of the Twelve (Minor Prophets) wanted Amos to be read in the light of the later Joel materials.

No clue for dating Joel's prophecies is given in the introductory verse to the book. But internal evidence lends strong support for a date around 400 BC. The fact that neither Assyria nor Babylon are mentioned implies that their dominance in Judah had long since passed. Judah's defeat and Exile in Babylon belonged to ancient history from Joel's perspective (Joel 3:1-3). The Temple (completed in 515 BC) and Jerusalem's walls (finished in 445 BC) are referred to casually as though restored for some time. Mention of the Greeks, but not as a world power, may be an argument for a date earlier than Alexander's conquests (336–332 BC). Leadership by elders and priests and a stable religious community imply a date following the Ezra-Nehemiah era. Joel's dependence on older prophets suggests a late date for his ministry. Much of his language is common to post-Exilic literature.

Joel's prophecies may be divided into two major sections: 1:1 to 2:27, with the focus on current circumstances; and 2:28 to 3:21, concerned with the future. Chapter divisions between the Hebrew and Greek texts vary. Chapter 1 is the same in both. Chapter 2 in Hebrew is chapter 2:1-27 in Greek. Chapter 3 in Hebrew is chapter 2:28-32 in Greek. Chapter 4 in Hebrew is chapter 3 in Greek. The Greek chapter arrangement is followed by English translations.

The Day of the Locusts
1:1 to 2:27

Joel called his countrymen to true repentance in view of the devastating judgment of God by the locust plague. Not with an outward ritual but with a rending of their hearts, citizens of Judah must return to God. Only then could they expect God's protection, restoration, and blessing.

Title (1:1)

The introductory verse indicates the nature of the material: It is Yahweh's word. It authenticates Joel as a bona fide prophet: Yahweh's word "came" (happened) to him. It affirms Joel's message to be authoritative: It came from God. "Joel" is a confessional name meaning "Yahweh is God." The absence of a date notice in the title verse probably indicates that Joel's ministry came after the fall of Israel and Judah.

Unprecedented Locust Plague (1:2-4)

A destructive locust plague formed the occasion for the word of the Lord to come to Joel. The plague was followed by a drought (vv. 19-20) which led naturally to famine. In that setting, Joel issued a call to lamentation.

"You aged men" does not necessarily designate the technical role of elder here (v. 2). Joel addressed the old ones because they had observed many locust plagues through the years. However, the fact that "aged men" is matched in the next line by "inhabitants of the land" may be reason enough to interpret "aged men" as a leadership group (compare 1:14 and 2:16). The imperative form of the verbs, "hear" and "give ear," reveals the prophet's earnest desire to get the attention of his audience. Everyone in Judah and Jerusalem, people and leaders alike, should listen to the prophet's message.

The expected answer to the rhetorical questions in verse 2 is No. Locust plagues had struck the land before, but in the memory of Joel's audience none had been so destructive as this one. The current crisis was unique. Joel's command to "tell" future generations about the plague implies that nothing like it would ever happen again. The plague was a sign of the approaching "day of the Lord" (v. 15). That is why future generations should be told about it (v. 3).

The unique "thing" referred to in veiled references earlier (vv. 2-3) is now identified specifically as a locust plague (v. 4). Joel's use of different names for the locusts does not seem to distinguish various species or stages of growth. Instead, the language suggests swarm after swarm of locusts. What one swarm left the next ate. With the triple use of "eaten" Joel pictured wave after wave of destruction until nothing was left. Probably more than one harvest was devoured (2:25). This account of total destruction is the starting point for the prophet's lament, his announcement of the day of the Lord, and his call to repentance.

Universal Mourning and Fasting (1:5-14)

"Drunkards" would be the first to experience loss from the locust plague (v. 5). For that reason, the prophet urged them to "awake" and "weep." Not only the alcoholics but all "drinkers of wine" would feel the pinch of loss. The prophet commanded them to "wail" as an appropriate response to the destruction wrought by the locusts. For the "drunkards" and the casual "drinkers" to have "the sweet wine" cut off from them would be a sobering experience. "Sweet wine" is literally "pressed out juice." Religious responses of weeping and wailing were appropriate because God was considered to be the one who gave or withheld the wine. Judah was God's land (v. 6), and its "vines" and "fig trees" were his (v. 7).

The locust plague is compared to an invading nation (v. 6). Normally the word rendered "nation" refers to foreign people. Here it designates locusts. "Powerful" and "without number" are practically synonymous. Both emphasize strength through large numbers. "Without number" is literally "there is no counting." The destructive power of the locusts is revealed by comparison of their teeth with "lions' teeth" and "fangs of a lioness" (v. 6b).

Verse 7 contains a vivid description of the devastation wrought by the locusts. "Vines" and "fig trees" were the two main fruit-bearing plants in Judah. These were destroyed—fruit, leaf, and bark. The locusts reduced the vines to waste and the fig trees to splinters. They stripped off the bark, leaving debris on the ground and the branches glistening white in the sun. What happened to the vines and fig trees is what would happen to Judah.

With a new command, Joel urged the nation to "lament" over the loss by the locust plague (v. 8). Added to weeping and wailing as signs of mourning is a new gesture of donning sackcloth. The distress caused by the locust attack is compared to the mourning of a "virgin" for "the bridegroom of her youth." In all probability, what is alluded to is the untimely and unexpected death of a man who has paid the bridal price for a wife but who has not taken her home. Death coming at that crucial time was considered especially cruel. "Sackcloth," a black cloth of woven goat's hair, served as a visible sign of mourning.

Part of the stress created by the locust plague was the threat to Temple services. The "cereal offering" was a combination of flour and oil, while the "drink offering" consisted of wine poured out to the Lord (v. 9). These were offered twice daily with the burnt offering (Ex. 29:38-42). Associated with the burnt offering was the assurance of salvation. The locust plague had put an end to these offerings. Priests mourned because they had clear insight into what the cessation of offerings meant. It signified that the people were out of fellowship with God and that the priests were without food. "Ministers of the Lord" designates the priests as caretakers of God's house, not personal servants of the Lord (compare v. 13).

"The ground" is personified as a participant in Judah's mourning (v. 10). It rejoices when the fields are productive (Ps. 65:12-13). But when "the grain is destroyed" (same word translated "laid waste" above), "the wine fails," and "the oil languishes," naturally the land mourns.

Joel commanded "tillers" and "vinedressers" to join in lamentation because the harvest of the field had failed (v. 11). "Wheat" and "barley" harvest were lost (v. 11); "vine," "fig tree," "pomegranate," "palm," and "apple," along with "all the trees of the field," withered (v. 12). Failing fields produced fading "gladness" among the inhabitants of Judah. And the culprits causing devastation and mourning were the locusts and the drought (compare vv. 19-20).

Finally Joel commanded "the priests" to engage in acts of mourning (v. 13) and to lead the people in appropriate religious acts (v. 14). With an economy of words, Joel's orders are "gird" (with sackcloth understood), "lament," "wail" (v. 13a). Mourners normally tore their garments, girded on sackcloth, beat their chests, let out

mournful wails, and, under extreme stress, passed the night in
sackcloth. The reason for the priests' lamentation is repeated
(compare v. 9): the daily offerings had ceased, and so had communion with God (v. 13b).

The prophet's commands to the priests are extended to include
their function of prescribing and leading the people to perform
appropriate ritual acts (v. 14). "Sanctify a fast" means "set apart a day
for fasting." A fast symbolized submission to a decreed calamity.
"Call a solemn assembly" probably means "announce rest from all
work." Both "elders" and "inhabitants" were to be gathered "to the
house of the Lord." Thus assembled, they were to "cry to the
Lord." The verb translated "cry" is always associated with fasting,
and fasting is usually related to some distressful situation.

Unsettling Portent of the Day of the Lord (1:15-18)

Joel saw the distress created by the locust plague and the drought
as an omen of the day of the Lord (v. 15). Apparently others did not
see what he saw. That is why he sent out a call to repentance
(2:12-14). "Day" does not mean a definite extent of time. It means a
definite event in time. And for Joel that event would not bring
salvation, blessing, and joy to Judah. "Alas for the day" is a cry of
alarm, terror, and distress.

"The day of the Lord" as an event in time was future to Joel. The
locust plague and drought had already happened, and the day of the
Lord was "near." But it had not arrived. In popular thought "the day
of the Lord" meant that Yahweh would intervene to put down
Israel's enemies and to establish Israel. Thus, it was generally
looked upon as a day of terror for Israel's enemies. Most of the
references to it in the prophetic materials show "the day of the
Lord" directed first against the nations (Israel's enemies) and then
against Israel. Only Zechariah (14:1,3) joins Joel in directing the day
first against God's people.

To show the similar sounding words of the original language in the
phrase "as destruction from the Almighty," some translators render
it, "as destruction from the Destroyer" (v. 15). Judah would
experience destruction, not deliverance, when the day arrived. The
form of the verb translated "it comes" suggests that the day was in
the process of coming. To Joel, the conditions facing Judah in the

wake of the locust plague and the drought revealed the nature and the nearness of the day of the Lord (vv. 16-18).

"Food" (or eating) was cut off and, as a result, "joy and gladness" were missing as usual sounds of worship in the Temple (v. 16). For want of moisture the "seed" failed to germinate, storehouses stood empty, and granaries were torn down (v. 17). "Herds" of large domestic animals and "flocks" of smaller animals were confused in their search for pasturage (v. 18). "Before our eyes" (v. 16) suggests that all these things were visible to any who had eyes to see. The lessons should have been obvious to all.

Urgent Appeal for the Lord's Help (1:19-20)

Joel summoned the elders and the inhabitants of Judah to a day of fasting and crying to God (v. 14). Now the prophet offers his own prayer of intercession (vv. 19-20). With emphatic language, "Unto thee, O Lord," he addressed his cry directly to God (v. 19). The verb rendered "cry" is not the distress cry of 1:14. It is the term regularly translated "call" and typically used of prayer under normal conditions. To the one who caused the distress and who alone could remove it, the prophet addressed his prayer. "For" introduces the cause of the distress which occasioned the prayer. "Fire" refers to the combined effect of the locusts and the drought. "Wilderness" denotes uncultivated ground suitable for feeding sheep. But fire had "devoured" the pastures and "burned" all the trees. Nothing was left for domestic animals.

So extreme was the distress that "wild beasts" longed for God to respond to their craving for water (v. 20). "Water brooks," their only source of drink, had dried up and "pastures," their only source of food, were eaten up. Thus Joel called attention to the fact that both man and beast suffered the ravages of locust and drought.

Unbearable Day of the Lord (2:1-11)

Again Joel announced the nearness of the approaching day of the Lord (v. 1). Then he expanded his earlier description of the plague as the forerunner of that day (vv. 2-11). He ordered the priests to alert the city to the impending danger by blowing a "trumpet," a wind instrument made from a ram's horn (v. 1). The alarm signal was to be sounded from "Zion," further identified as "my holy mountain." These references designate God's dwelling place. The urgency of the signal is indicated by the response of the "inhabitants." They are to "tremble" over the day of the Lord, not only because it is "coming" and is "near," but because it will be totally destructive. Joel described the day in words like those of Zephaniah and Amos (v. 2a): "darkness and gloom," "clouds and thick darkness." The day would bring evil, calamity, and adversity.

The coming of the locusts spread literal "blackness" (v. 2b), blocking out the light by their great numbers. Joel compared the locust attack to an invading army. "Great and powerful" means many and mighty. Their numbers and destructiveness were unparalleled in the past and would be in the future. Like a raging forest fire, the locusts ate up everything in their path (v. 3). Like a powerful army, equipped, disciplined, and determined, they were unstoppable (vv. 4-9). They looked like "war horses" (v. 4); they sounded like "chariots" and a raging "fire" (v. 5). They acted like "a powerful army" (people) (v. 5c), courageous "warriors," and disciplined "soldiers" (vv. 7-9).

Appropriately enough, "peoples" respond with intense anguish before the onslaught (v. 6); heaven and earth tremble, and sun, moon, and stars are darkened (v. 10). Here the prophet mixes apocalyptic images with the attacking army metaphors he used earlier to describe the locust plague.

At the helm of "his army," the Lord gives orders and executes his word (v. 11a). "Utters his voice" is literally "gives his voice (thunder)." "His host" (camp) refers to the locusts. "Exceedingly great" is literally "very many," noting the great horde of insects. God is endowed with adequate power to execute his word. As sovereign Lord he may use locusts to do it. Clearly Joel wanted his audience to understand that the announced distress over a locust plague only signaled the onset of the day of the Lord (v. 11b). He warned that that day was "great and very terrible" (compare Mal. 4:5). Then influenced perhaps by Zephaniah (1:14) he questioned, "Who can endure it?" The implied answer is, "No one."

Unconditional Return to the Lord (2:12-17)

Even under the extreme conditions just described, Joel offered Judah God's invitation to repent. The time was late, but not too late to return to God (v. 12). "Says the Lord" means that Yahweh himself is offering the nation a way out. The Lord's command to "return" implies that it is possible for Judah to turn to God for help. "Return to me with all your heart" means "repent sincerely." No halfway or halfhearted measure would do. Interestingly, Joel was not against Judah's use of customary rituals (fasting, weeping, mourning) to demonstrate outwardly their inward and wholehearted repentance.

Judah's repentance demanded more than torn garments as evidence of grief. They must present to God broken and contrite hearts to demonstrate the submission of their obstinate wills to him (v. 13). The basis of their repentance was the character of God. Joel's switch to third person references to God is explained by the fact that he began quoting Exodus 34:6-7 (compare Jonah 4:2). "Gracious" is that quality in God that inclines him to show favor where none is due. "Merciful" means the kind of tender compassion a mother shows for her child, or that brothers show for each other. "Slow to anger" is literally "long of nostrils." It means that God is patient even with sinners. "Abounding in steadfast love" describes God's overflowing, covenant-keeping, loyal love. "Repents of evil" suggests that God breathes a sigh of relief that the announced judgment does not have to be carried out.

God's character has been described (v. 13). Now with the question his absolute freedom is declared (v. 14). God's character would dispose him to "repent" upon man's return. But it is not automatic. Man's return does not guarantee it. God is completely free to "turn and repent," and, as a token that he has, "leave a blessing behind him." For worshipers to present "a cereal offering and a drink offering" would require that God first leave a blessing for them. That is, he would have to give relief from the plague and the drought to make their fields and vineyards fruitful.

Verses 15-17 contain instructions to carry out the call to repentance. Flight from the enemy (2:1) should lead to refuge in God (2:15). The priest's function was to make full preparations for a "fast." This involved setting apart a day, releasing the people from work, gathering the people for the ritual, and leading them in it. The whole congregation must be involved in the fast. No exceptions were to be allowed (v. 16b). The priest's appeal for God to "spare" (pity) his people was based on Judah's covenant relationship to God (v. 17). "Heritage" is parallel to "people." It identifies God's people as his possession. "Make not" is literally "give not." "A byword among the nations" is literally "to rule over them, nations." No greater reproach could come to God's people than for them to be ruled over by the nations. In mockery of Judah and their God, the nations would question "Where is their God?" What kind of a God is a God who cannot take care of his own people?

Unrestricted Promises of Restoration (2:18-27)

The genuine repentance of God's people stirred him to "jealous" (zealous) anger for "his land" (v. 18a). Thus he "had pity" (spared) on "his people" (v. 18b). God's answer (response) to the plea of his people would be twofold: (1) "grain, wine and oil" to satisfy their hunger; and (2) a pledge never to give them as "a reproach among the nations" (v. 19). The locust plague (harbinger of the day of the Lord) would be removed (v. 20); fear would be over, and joy would be restored (v. 21); refreshing rain would give relief to people and beasts alike (vv. 22-23); and bountiful harvests would make up for the lean years (vv. 24-26). Again Judah would "know" the protection and the benefits of God's presence in their midst. Yahweh alone would be acknowledged as their God. Judah would never again be put to shame (v. 27).

The Day of the Lord
2:28 to 3:21

God's presence and blessing would answer the plea of his people in the present time (2:18-27). But what about the future? The "afterward" of 2:28 forms the transition to the rest of the book where God's promises for a more distant time are discussed (2:28 to 3:21).

Prediction of Spiritual Illumination (2:28-29)

In the midst of his people God would "pour out his spirit" on them (v. 28). "Spirit" (wind) is vital power from God to sustain the life of his feeble people. Their "sons" and "daughters," "old men" and "young men," as well as "menservants" and "maidservants," would be recipients of the "spirit" (vv. 28b-29). Moses had longed for this (Num. 11:29). Nothing in the context indicates that these "prophets" would proclaim anything, or attempt to evangelize the nations. The meaning seems to be that each person in Judah would stand in a relationship of immediacy to God. Peter universalized this prophecy (Acts 2:17-21).

Deliverance of the Faithful (2:30-32)

God promised "portents in the heavens and on the earth" (v. 30) as warnings to the faithful of the approaching day of the Lord. The word rendered "portents" (wonders) was used to describe God's acts in Egypt which preceded Israel's release from bondage (Ex. 7:3). In Scripture such signs frequently precede great events. Here the sun turned to darkness and the moon to blood would serve as God's signs that the great and terrible day of the Lord approached (v. 31). In that setting God promised deliverance for all who would call on his name (v. 32). The verb rendered "delivered" is usually translated "escape." To call on the "name" of the Lord is to base the plea for deliverance on God's character, purpose, and will. Joel's promise of "Zion"/"Jerusalem" as the place of escape must have been a conscious quote from Obadiah (v. 17). But Joel makes very clear that it is not physical membership among the people of this place which brings deliverance. Escape is for those who respond to God's call.

Judgment upon Israel's Enemies (3:1-3)

"For" (v. 1) indicates that "in those days and at that time" is connected with chapter 2 where the day of the Lord as a day of deliverance for Judah is discussed (2:30-32). Clearly the Lord will be responsible for Judah's escape. "Restore the fortunes" is literally "return the returnings."

Restoration for Judah and Jerusalem and judgment for "the nations" would be two sides of "the day of the Lord." An intensive form of the verb "gather" expresses the force and the intensity of God's determined purpose to assemble the nations (v. 2). The form of the verb translated "bring them down" is even more forceful. "The valley of Jehoshaphat" has been identified (from the fourth century AD) with the valley between Jerusalem and the Mount of

Olives. That valley is called Kidron in the New Testament. "Jehoshaphat" means "Yahweh judges" and is used to emphasize the person who judges, not the place of judgment. That emphasis is made clear by the word play between "Jehoshaphat" (Yahweh judges) and the next word translated "I will enter into judgment."

God was gathering the nations for judgment because of what they had done to "Israel" (v. 2b). For Joel "Israel" is synonymous with Judah. "My people" and "my heritage" are covenant terms. "Israel" was God's possession. The nations had "scattered them," "divided" the land, and made slaves of them. In a series of deportations, God's people had been scattered by the Assyrians (733 and 722 BC) and the Babylonians (597 and 586 BC). The nations had "divided up" God's "land" to foreigners after the fall of Jerusalem in 586 BC. They "cast lots" to decide who would get God's "people" as slaves. Boys and girls were degraded to the level of trade items. "A boy for a harlot" (or the price to cover the charges of one night with a harlot) and "a girl for wine" (or the price to cover the charges of a drunken party) are humiliating evaluations of human lives.

Punishment of Tyre, Sidon, and Philistia (3:4-8)

With legal language in the form of questions, the general charges made in verses 1-3 are now particularized. "Tyre and Sidon," Phoenician cities northwest of Jerusalem, and "regions [circles] of Philistia," five city states west of Jerusalem, had plundered God's defeated people. They took "silver and gold" to embellish their temples (v. 5). They seized and sold citizens of Judah as slaves to the "Greeks" (v. 6). Now the tables would be turned. God would return those slaves of Judah to their own land (v. 7), sell Phoenician and Philistine sons to Judah, and Judah would sell them as slaves to the Sabeans (v. 8).

Summons of the Nations to the Day of the Lord (3:9-17)

Initially, the summons is for the nations to prepare for battle (v. 9). Later the call is sharpened to mean a gathering for judgment (v. 12). The urgency of the summons is expressed in a series of imperative verbs. God's messengers are ordered to "proclaim" (call) the summons "among the nations" (v. 9). The nations are ordered to "prepare [sanctify] war." Apparently this involved prayers and offerings (1 Sam. 7:8-10). The term translated "mighty men", designates soldiers or warriors. These strong men are identified as "men of war" in the next line and instructed to "draw near" and "come up" in battle readiness. These two verbs describe an army's advance into battle.

Verse 10 is in sharp contrast with Isaiah 2:4 and Micah 4:3. The size and significance of the announced battle will require the use of every possible weapon and every available warrior. Tools for farming and vinedressing must be converted to implements of war and "the weak" who would be exempt ordinarily must volunteer for service. The term translated "warrior" is a singular form of the word rendered "mighty men" in verse 9. With strong commands, "hasten and come," the nations are urged to gather at the battle site. "There" seems to refer to the valley of Jehoshaphat (3:2). Verse 12 confirms that location. Finally the enemy of "the nations" is identified as the Lord's "warriors" (v. 11c).

The summons which seemed to be a call to battle (vv. 9-10) is now revealed to be a gathering for judgment (v. 12). The "nations" would "come" concerned for war. But God would "sit" concerned for justice. The Lord's "warriors" (v. 11c) are ordered to take punitive action against the nations (v. 13). "Sickle" is probably a knife used by a vinedresser, since the context clearly portrays a grape harvest. It is time to put in the sickle because "the harvest is ripe." It is urgent to "go in" and "tread" because "the wine press is full." The third line interprets the first two. The vats overflow because they are filled with the great "wickedness" of the nations. They are ripe for judgment.

What the prophet heard and what he saw signaled the nearness of the day of the Lord (vv. 14-15). The noise of multitudes gathering in the valley of decision (v. 14) and the apocalyptic signs visible in the heavens (v. 15) were his clues. Both verbs in verse 15 suggest the certainty and the proximity of the day of the Lord. Verse 16a seems to be a direct quote from Amos 1:2a. Joel took the threat which Amos directed against Israel and turned it against the nations. The word of God is charged with such authority and energy that "the heavens and the earth shake." But "his people" need not fear, for he is "a refuge" (shield) and "a stronghold" (bulwark) for them.

By God's intervention on the day of the Lord, Israel would "know" (recognize, acknowledge) Yahweh as their God. His dwelling place in "Zion"/"Jerusalem" is "holy." Thus all "strangers"

(foreign nations) who would defile it would be excluded. At last
God's people would be at peace.

Promises of Restoration for Judah (3:18-21)

Joel's conception of the day of the Lord as a day of defeat for
Israel's enemies and a day of deliverance for Israel is summarized
and supplemented in 3:18-21. Not only would Judah find refuge and
deliverance in God (v. 16), but also the nation would enjoy paradisal
abundance "in that day" (v. 18). An extravagantly fruitful land would
follow the decision in the valley (v. 14). Similar language is used in
Amos 9:13 to picture overflowing abundance in the end time.

Obviously the Lord is the source of fruitfulness in Judah (v. 18).
His relationship to the abounding supply of "wine," "milk," and
"water" is indicated by the reference to "a fountain" that shall "come
forth from the house of the Lord" (compare Ezek. 47:1-12; Zech.
14:8). A literal translation reveals Joel's emphasis: "a fountain from
the house of the Lord shall go out." This figurative description must
have influenced the vision reported in Revelation 22:1. The mes-
sianic hope in Joel's prophecy would be fulfilled "in that day."

Egypt and Edom, longtime foes of Israel, may stand for all of the
nation's opponents. God the righteous judge would not only deliver
and bless Judah, but he would also judge Judah's enemies (v. 19).
They had done "violence" to Judah. Now God would make them a
"desolation." Probably no specific event is intended in Joel's reference to shedding "innocent blood in their land." Both Edom (Obad.
9-14) and Egypt (2 Kings 14:25-26) were guilty of such a charge.

In contrast with Egypt and Edom, made desolate by God's
judgment, Judah would be "inhabited for ever" (v. 20) and
Jerusalem would continue as the capital city generation after
generation. The final verse contains God's promise to "avenge"
Judah's blood. Fulfillment of that promise is as certain as the fact
that Yahweh "dwells in Zion" (v. 21). Joel ended his prophecies with
the most reassuring promise in all the Bible, "the Lord dwells in
Zion."

AMOS

Introduction

Amos, Hosea, Isaiah, and Micah made up the quartet of eighth-century BC prophets. Amos and Hosea ministered in the Northern Kingdom of Israel, while Isaiah and Micah ministered in the Southern Kingdom of Judah. Amos was from Tekoa in Judah, but served as a prophet to Israel. Amos is usually designated the first of the classical (writing) prophets. His materials were collected, preserved, and passed on because of the new element he introduced into prophecy. That new element was the announcement of Israel's doom. God's judgment upon his elect nation would mean the end of the kingdom of Israel.

The Prophet

Amos's name means "burdened," or "burden bearer." It is from a verbal root that means "load," or "carry a load." He certainly carried a weighty word from God. However, he was a layman, a shepherd, and a dresser of sycamore trees, until God tapped him for prophetic ministry (7:14). His hometown was Tekoa in Judah about ten miles south of Jerusalem and some eighteen miles west of the Dead Sea. His two occupations put him in touch with numerous sources of information about other nations.

Amos denied any association with the guild of prophets (7:14). Instead, his calling came directly from God. With courage and conviction, he delivered God's message to Israel. He interpreted the lion's roar of God's voice and the shaking of the earth by an earthquake as symbols of God's destructive judgment upon his people. The day of the Lord would arrive as a lion's roar and as earthquake time for Israel, a day of darkness and not light.

The Period

Amos' ministry may be dated some time during the reign of Jeroboam II in Israel (787-746 BC). The reference in the superscription (1:1) to "two years before the earthquake" offers no help in pinpointing his ministry. But this notation may be a sound clue by which to limit the length of Amos' ministry. "Two years before the earthquake" would seem to mean some time during the year designated by the reference. Internal evidence in the Book of Amos would lend support to the period of peace and prosperity during Jeroboam II's reign as the general time of Amos' ministry.

A date for Amos' ministry near 760 BC is suggested by a number of factors: (1) archaeological evidence of an earthquake at Hazor about 760 BC; (2) scientific evidence for an eclipse of the sun visible to this area in 763 BC (8:9); (3) Amos' failure to mention Assyria as a threat to Israel, indicating a period before that source of threat became evident (about 745 BC); and (4) the absence of Jotham from the list of kings in the superscription, indicating that his coregency (about 757 BC) with Uzziah had not begun.

The times were good when Amos launched his prophetic ministry. Political stability under Jeroboam II brought an era of peace and prosperity. No enemy from without threatened the tranquility and well-being of Israel's citizens. The rash of political assassinations and consequent chaos prevalent in Hosea's time (about 750-725 BC) was in the future. But the times were bad in less observable ways. Prosperity was real, but it was only the rich who were getting richer. The poor were getting poorer. The rich built larger and larger estates by confiscation of land from poor debtors, through bribery of the judges, and by intimidation of witnesses. Ritualistic activity was at a fever pitch as prosperous merchants and landowners gathered to thank their obliging God.

The Prophecies

Amos' prophetic materials may be divided into two basic categories: words, chapters 1—6; and visions, chapters 7—9. The superscription seems to acknowledge these two divisions in the terms translated "words" and "which he saw." The oracles in 1:3 to 2:16 are introduced as Yahweh's word. The messages in chapters 3—6 are a mingling of Yahweh's words and Amos' words.

The five vision reports in the second division of the book are found in 7:1-8; 8:1-3; and 9:1-4. Other kinds of material found in Amos are: (1) doxologies, 4:13; 5:8-9; 9:5-6; (2) a third person narrative, 7:10-17; (3) woe sayings, 5:18-20; 6:1-3,4-7; and (4) an eschatological vision, 9:11-15.

Amos may not have been a "man of letters" but he was a master literary technician. Evidences for his effective use of language include the following: (1) word plays, 6:1,7; 8:1-3; (2) series, 1:3 to 2:16; 4:6-12; and (3) metaphors, 1:2; 4:1. The prophet employed all of his literary skills to communicate one message: announcement of the end of Israel.

The Words of Amos
1:1 to 6:14

Superscription and Theme (1:1-2)

Verses 1 and 2 give respectively the title and the theme of the book. The book is composed of sayings, "words," spoken by "Amos." The speaker is identified as to occupation, "among the shepherds," and geographical location, "Tekoa" in Judah. That Amos was a resident of Judah is confirmed in 7:12. "Shepherd" designates Amos as a sheep breeder, not an ordinary shepherd. "Which he saw" reveals the method by which the prophet received the "words" from God. They were God's words before they became Amos's words. These words were for "Israel." The term rendered "concerning" may as properly be translated "against."

A general date notice puts Amos's ministry in the time when Uzziah was king in Judah (783-742 BC) and when Jeroboam II was king in Israel (787-746 BC). A more precise dating must be intended by the phrase "two years before the earthquake." Those who first received the message from Amos probably knew which earthquake "the earthquake" designated. Archaeologists have identified considerable damage at Hazor from an earthquake they would date in 760 BC. Perhaps this is the one referred to in the superscription and again in Zechariah 14:5.

The first message sets the tone for the entire book (v. 2). "The Lord" (Yahweh) and "from Zion" are placed ahead of the verb for emphasis. In the next line "from Jerusalem" comes before the verb to stress the source of God's voice. The Lord himself is the speaker whose terrifying voice has the power to destroy. His voice is compared to a lion's roar. Amos experienced that voice personally when he recognized that God had called him for prophetic ministry (3:8). As a shepherd Amos knew the awful roar of a fierce lion attacking the flock.

The power of God's voice may be seen in the devastating effect it had on the land. Two targets affected by God's powerful roar were "the pastures of the shepherds" and "the top of Carmel." As by a searing drought, the pastures "mourn" and Carmel "withers."

God's Controversy with the Nations (1:3 to 2:3)

The series of eight oracles (1:3 to 2:16) was not delivered to each of the nations indicated, as is clear from the third person references to them. Only in the oracle against Israel is direct address used, "I brought you up" (2:10-11). The audience for all the oracles was a gathering of Israelites, probably for some regular festival event. Amos gained a powerful psychological advantage for his message to Israel by using as his introduction the strong condemnation of surrounding nations.

Each oracle is an announcement of judgment. The basic structure consists of (1) the messenger formula, (2) the indictment, (3) the announcement of judgment, and (4) a concluding messenger formula. The fourth element is missing from the oracles against Tyre, Edom, and Judah. The oracle against Israel begins with the first two elements, except that the indictment is expanded. Then the formula is abandoned altogether. The rhythmical repetition of the series has a cumulative effect. Amos's audience must have listened approvingly to the oracles condemning their traditional enemies. But when he inserted the name of their sister kingdom to the south into his formula, he probably got their undivided attention. The climax came when the prophet named Israel as the target of God's devastating judgment.

The first oracle is against Damascus, the capital of Aram (Syria), on Israel's northeastern border. Almost constant border wars characterized Israel's relationship to Damascus from the middle of the ninth century BC to the beginning of the eighth. The indictment in verse 3 is the basis for the judgment announced in verses 4 and 5. Amos used the graduated numerical saying, common in the literature of Israel's neighbors and in her own wisdom materials, as the vehicle for the indictment. The numerical sequence in other literature may range from one-two to nine-ten. Amos chose three-four, the sequence found most often elsewhere. "Three" means enough; "four" means more than enough. "Three" is full; "four" is an overflow. Amos believed that "transgression" in a nation could reach a saturation point. That point is represented here by "three." To that point God's patience and long-suffering might go. But transgression beyond that point would surely bring down the judgment of God upon such a nation. Only the fourth transgression is named (v. 3c).

The term translated "transgression" means rebellion against constituted authority. According to Amos, the surrounding nations were just as accountable as Israel for breaches of God's universally valid laws. The sin of Damascus had gone beyond God's tolerance level. "I will not revoke the punishment" is literally "not will I cause it to return." Some interpreters take "it" to be the Lord's "voice" in verse 2. Others think the reference is to the threat of judgment implied by the overflow of sin (vv. 4-5).

Cruelty in warfare was the overflow of transgression for Damascus (v. 3c). "Gilead" probably designates the territory north of the Jabbok, bordering the Aramean kingdom. Ordinarily "threshing sledges of iron" were used to thresh grain. Sharp iron prongs studded the underside of the sledges. That which was normally drawn over grain to thresh it may have been drawn over prisoners of war to mangle their flesh.

God would personally direct the judgment upon Damascus (vv. 4-5). "Fire" came to be a symbol for war because use of fire was a chief strategy of warfare. Only one Hazael of Damascus is mentioned in the Old Testament (2 Kings 8:7-15). He murdered the reigning Ben-hadad and ruled from 842 to 806 BC. The new dynasty he founded was known in Assyrian writings as the "house of Hazael." Hazael's son and successor was named Ben-hadad (2 Kings 13:3), possibly the king Amos referred to. His reign extended into the eighth century. "Strongholds" served a dual purpose: as a secure refuge and as a treasure house. God's "fire" would "devour" (eat) Ben-hadad's strongholds. War would level these places of pride and protection.

God's judgment upon Syria would include breaking "the bar of Damascus." The "bar" was the locking device by which the city gate was secured. To "break the bar" would expose the inhabitants to the attack of an enemy. Other regions beyond Damascus would be affected by God's judgment. The names "Valley of Aven" and "Beth-eden" characterize the regions. The first means "sin valley," and the second is literally "house of pleasure." God threatened to "cut off" (cut down like trees) the respective rulers of these districts. "Him that holds the scepter" designates the ruler. The general reference to inhabitants is in the last line. God's judgment upon "the people of Syria" is "exile to Kir." Amos named Kir as the original home of the Syrians (9:7).

Into the form established in the first oracle, the names of other people, their overflowing sin, and God's sure judgment are inserted. "Gaza" represents the league of Philistine cities to the southwest of Israel (vv. 6-8). Their overflowing transgression was slave trade, a common practice associated with war. The cruelty of taking captives into exile was heightened by two factors. To carry "a whole people" (the entire population) into exile left no hope for repopulation. Then insult was added to injury when they handed over such defenseless people to a third party. Who the "whole people" were is left open (possibly Judah or Israel), but Edom is named as the recipient (or middleman) of Gaza's cruel act. Slave trade is not named as Edom's overflowing sin (v. 11).

God's personal involvement in the judgment announced for Gaza and the other Philistine city-states is made clear by the first person verbs (vv. 7-8). With "fire" (war) he would "devour" Gaza's "strongholds" (v. 7). He would "cut off" the respective rulers of Ashdod and Ashkelon. His "hand" (power) would be against Ekron and the only future "the remnant of the Philistines" could anticipate would be to "perish." Gath is left out of the list of Philistine cities, probably because it had come under the rule of Judah or Ashdod.

The oracle against Tyre follows the general pattern already established (vv. 9-10), except that it is brief. No other Phoenician cities are named in the announced judgment, and the concluding messenger formula is omitted. Tyre's transgression is similar to Gaza's. They too "delivered up a whole people to Edom" (v. 9). The difference was that Tyre broke "a covenant of brotherhood." God's announced judgment against Tyre would be destruction of their defenses and treasures by "fire" (war). Alexander the Great conquered Tyre in 333 BC by building a causeway over from the mainland to the island.

The hostility between Esau (Edom) and Jacob began before birth, persisted in their lives, and continued through their offspring. The indictment against Edom is that "he pursued his brother with the sword" (v. 11). Amos' audience knew that Jacob (Israel) was "his brother." The particular historical event alluded to is not clear. It could have been any one of many such evidences of hatred between these two brother kingdoms. Edom "cast off all pity." "Pity," fellow womb-sharing compassion, should have controlled Edom's actions. Instead, "anger" dominated the Edomite response to Jerusalem's helpless plight. They plundered the city, took captives and sold them into slavery (Obad. 13-14).

The brunt of God's judgment upon Edom would be focused upon two chief cities (or regions): Teman and Bozrah (v. 12). The two names probably designate regions since "upon the wall" is missing. "Fire" (war) was the instrument of judgment, and destruction of their "strongholds" was the result.

The oracle against "the Ammonites" (sons of Ammon) is fully developed (vv. 13-15). Ammon was one of Lot's sons and, therefore, related to God's chosen people through Abraham (Gen. 19:30-38). They dwelt on the east side of the Jordan and north of Moab. "Rabbah" was the capital city. Their overflowing transgression was an atrocity of war. They "ripped up women with child in Gilead" (v. 13). Border wars aimed at terrorizing and decimating the population frequently included this horrible practice. For the Ammonites, the purpose was territorial expansion, "that they might enlarge their border."

God's judgment by "fire" would destroy the strongholds of the capital city (v. 14). Instead of the usual "send fire," the language here is "kindle a fire" (compare Jer. 17:27). "Shouting" designates the chaotic, excited battle cries of men engaged in fierce warfare. The term translated "tempest" is usually used in contexts describing a theophany (Isa. 29:6). God's approach would bring destruction as "in the day of the whirlwind."

One result of God's judgment upon Ammon would be the deportation of "their king" and "his princes" (v. 15). The two chief features of God's judgment upon Damascus and Gaza, removal of royal power and destruction of military defenses, characterize this oracle against Ammon.

Moab's territory touched the land of Ammon on the north and that of Edom on the south. It lay east of the Dead Sea. Moabites and Ammonites were related to Israel in the same way, through Abraham's nephew Lot. The indictment against Moab is that "he burned to lime the bones of the king of Edom" (2:1). When this was done and to what Edomite king is unknown. Did the Moabites capture and burn alive some Edomite king? Or did they capture, kill, and burn the remains of the king? Or did they exhume the body of some deceased king and desecrate his remains by burning them? The last suggestion is the most likely one.

God's "fire" (war) upon Moab would destroy the defenses of Kerioth (v. 2). According to a Moabite inscription, Kerioth was the site of a shrine to Chemosh, the Moabite God. Israelites would have delighted in God's defeat of a city dedicated to the worship of a pagan god. The judgment of war upon Moab is described with sound-words related to combat. "Uproar" is the sound made by hordes of storming soldiers (Isa. 13:4). The general population of Moab would die amid the terrifying sounds of war: "uproar," "shouting," and the blast of the "trumpet."

Moab's "ruler" and "princes" would be eliminated (v. 3). God himself threatened to "cut off" the ruler and "slay" the princes. The term translated "ruler" is usually rendered "judge." But matched with "princes" it must be a synonym for king.

God's Controversy with His Own People (2:4-16)

Some interpreters suggest that this oracle, along with the ones against Tyre and Edom, did not originate with Amos. Their claim is that the language and style betray a time around 621 BC. However, the inclusion of Judah in the oracles should not surprise anyone, since their sins were very nearly the same as Israel's (compare Isa. 1).

Judah's indictment is not for war crimes, but "because they have rejected the law of the Lord" (2:4). The verb translated "rejected" may be rendered as correctly "despised." "Law" may refer to the instructions given by the priests or to a collection of laws. To despise, lightly esteem, or reject the priest's instruction or the body of accepted stipulations is ultimately to reject God. The noun translated "statutes" is derived from a verb that means to cut in, or engrave. It usually designates inscriptions on a rock or tablet. Here the term likely refers to ritual laws. God charged Judah with not keeping or observing these laws.

The final part of the indictment against Judah is a charge of idolatry. This use of "lies" to mean false gods or idolatry is unique to Amos. But set over against rejection of Yahweh's "law" and considering the language used to describe their "lies," no other alternative is open. "Have led them astray" is literally "have caused them to err." With the mention of "their fathers" previous generations are indicted along with the current one for practicing idolatry.

The same pattern of judgment by war is announced for Judah. Rejection of Yahweh's word and practice of idolatry must be considered equal to (or worse than) atrocities of war. The same fate awaiting the other nations awaited Judah. Other nations sinned in midnight darkness. Judah sinned in midday light.

The final oracle begins just like the others with the messenger formula, "thus says the Lord" (2:6). Then Amos used the exact words already established as the pattern to set forth the indictment against the nation being charged. No doubt the prophet gained the full attention of his audience when he inserted the name "Israel" into the formula. For Amos the name "Israel" meant more than the national entity of the Northern Kingdom and their royal court. It meant people of God.

The charge against Israel is not rejection of "the law" in general, but breach of specific laws (vv. 6b-8). Up to this point only one "transgression" has been named in the oracles. Some interpreters think Amos charged Israel with only one overflowing transgression, namely oppression of the poor. Others find four sins: injustice, immorality, idolatry, and intemperance. However one counts the transgressions, the indictment against Israel is the longest one of all.

The first part of Israel's overflowing transgression involves the illegal sale of people into slavery (v. 6b). The "righteous" are the ones in the right in a legal suit. They are the innocent ones whom the court should vindicate. Persons became slaves in the ancient Near East by being captured in warfare and by being sold for debts. People were sold for money (silver) or for property (symbolized by a pair of sandals) to satisfy debts owed to wealthy creditors. The article attached to the word translated "silver" means a specified amount of silver.

Perhaps the barb in Israel's transgression was the perversion of justice. Or it might have been the selling of persons (innocent at that) as though they were things. The "needy" (persons with unfulfilled desires) in the next line match the "righteous" in this line. In the same way "a pair of shoes" is parallel to "silver." "A pair of shoes" may mean for a pittance, while the "silver" could stand for a relatively large sum. If "a pair of shoes" is symbolic of property exchange, then the value could be extremely high. It would mean that the poor man's property was appropriated by the rich creditor.

Oppression of the poor by the rich is the subject of the charge in verse 7a. The term translated "poor" means weak, thin, or helpless. Parallel to "poor" in the next line is the word rendered "the afflicted." The essential idea in this matching word is to be bowed down, or humbled. "The afflicted" are those who have been humbled by adverse circumstances. The form of the verb translated "they that trample" suggests an activity going on continuously and in present time. This vicious persecution by the rich crushed the head of the poor "into the dust of the earth."

To "turn aside the way" means to pervert justice. The next part of the charge against Israel concerns moral sin, or perhaps the combination of moral and cultic sins (v. 7b). "Maiden" denotes a marriageable girl. The sin charged against Israel centers neither upon the age nor upon the status of the maiden. Of focal concern is the fact that "a man and his father" consort sexually with "the same maiden." We are not told the circumstances of how this came about. However, we are told that this "profaned" God's "holy name."

The next two lines in verse 8 are connected with the last part of verse 7. "They" (v. 8) has "a man and his father" (v. 7) as the antecedent. Also, the words "altar" and "house of their God" (v. 8) are related to "my holy name" (v. 7). Some sin of worship seems to be indicated. Perhaps what is meant is that a man and his father frequented pagan altars. They joined in the fertility rites associated with worship at such sites. They used "garments taken in pledge" in their practice of immorality "beside every altar." Israel's law required that such garments be returned to the debtor before night (Ex. 22:26 ff.). Their "drink" for those festive occasions was the wine of those who had been fined.

All the items listed in the indictment of Israel represent some act of oppression against the poor. And much of it was done in the name of religion. It was the poor who were sold into slavery for debts they could not pay. It was the poor who suffered when justice was perverted. The "maiden" may have been the daughter of a poor debtor sold to repay her father's debt. It was the poor who suffered because their garments were taken in pledge for debts owed. It was the poor who payed their fines with wine. And it was the rich who benefited in every case.

In the place of the usual announcement of God's judgment following the indictment, Amos recited some of God's saving acts in Israel's behalf. God's saving acts are in sharp contrast with Israel's sinful acts. The inhabitants of Canaan were called Amorites (v. 9). Their size and strength were proverbial. They were tall like "cedars" and strong like "oaks." But they were not too tall for God to cut down, nor were they too strong for God to subdue. To destroy the "fruit above" would leave no hope of life and growth from seed. To destroy the "roots beneath" would leave no hope for life and growth from sprouts.

Why the prophet listed the destruction of the Amorite (v. 9) before the deliverance from Egypt (v. 10) is a mystery. One possibility is that the loss of the Land of Promise was at stake. God worked at both ends to free Israel from the strong Egyptians on the one hand and to free the land from the powerful Amorites on the other. And in between he did not abandon them in the wilderness, but provided for all their needs. Once they were in the land, God "raised up . . . prophets" to bring them his word and "Nazirites" to model his way (v. 11). Israel had no excuse for the practice of such sins as those listed in the indictment. Amos wanted to elicit such an acknowledgement from his audience with the concluding question in verse 11: "Is it not indeed so, O people of Israel?"

God's gracious provision of prophets and Nazirites was the basis for an additional indictment against Israel (v. 12). Nazirites abstained from cutting their hair, drinking wine, and touching dead bodies (Num. 6:1-8). They were models of moderation in an age of indulgence. The "prophets" were mediums of the revelation of God's will. Most Israelites found the Nazirites and the prophets to be intolerable. They forced the Nazirites to drink wine and commanded the prophets not to prophesy. Amos knew firsthand about the latter (7:13,16).

God's judgment against Israel is described in verses 13-16. Fire is not mentioned here, but a complete military rout is portrayed. A cart overloaded with sheaves is the metaphor Amos selected to picture God's judgment upon his people. Either God felt the weight of

Israel's sin as a burden he had to bear (King James Version), or Israel would feel the weight of God's severe judgment bearing down upon them (Revised Standard Version).

The verb (used only here) translated "press" may mean "cleave." As an overloaded cart cleaves the soft earth of the field, so God's judgment will come upon Israel in the form of an earthquake. Amos's fourth (8:1-2) and fifth (9:1-4) visions employ the images of harvest and earthquake to picture God's judgment.

What follows the announcement of God's severe judgment (v. 13) a description of panic as Israel's army confronts the Almighty (vv. 14-16). The swift would not be able to flee fast enough; the strong would not be able to muster strength enough; the mighty soldier sent to defend the populace would not be able to save his own life (v. 14). Those skilled in using the bow would not be able to prevail even with superior weaponry; the runner and the one riding a horse would be unable to escape (v. 15). Even the most courageous soldiers would simply drop their armor and their implements of war and flee (v. 16).

"In that day" is when the horror and panic described in verses 14-16 would prevail. "That day" is probably a short form of "the day of the Lord" (5:18-20). The "day" would usher in Israel's defeat. That is the message Amos heard Yahweh speak, as the concluding divine oracle formula indicates.

Privilege and Responsibility (3:1-15)

Verses 1 and 2 of chapter 3 fit better as the basis of the judgment messages in the rest of the chapter than as a conclusion to chapters 1 and 2. Because God chose Israel to stand in a privileged relationship to him, the nation is more responsible than the rest of the nations. This message is not introduced by the messenger formula but in words typical of a teacher of the law, "hear this word." The verb is an imperative form, demanding the attentiveness of the hearers. "This word" points ahead to the brief message in verse 2.

Amos used the verb translated "has spoken" when he wanted to stress the significance of the act of Yahweh's speaking (v. 1a; compare 3:8). And the word Amos heard Yahweh speak was "against" Israel, not for them. "O people of Israel" designates the hearers in their identity as God's people, not simply as the Northern Kingdom. Use of "the whole family" in the second part of verse 1 makes that identification clear. The saving act of God, the keystone of Israel's election, included "the whole family," not just the Northern Kingdom. God is the one who "brought up [Israel] from Egypt." Thus, they belonged to God. They needed to understand themselves, their sins, and God's judgment upon them in the light of their election.

The election of Israel is emphasized by two phrases: "You only" (placed in the emphatic position in the sentence) and "of all the families of the earth" (which sets the election in a worldwide context). "Have I known" is a covenant term, relational rather than cognitive. God knew all the nations in a cognitive sense. But he recognized Israel only from among all the nations in the special covenant relationship.

The form of the verb translated "have I known" suggests a completed fact in the past. To know meant to recognize legally in vassal treaties used among Hittites and Akkadians in the time of Amos. Because God recognized Israel "only" as his covenant partner, they alone were responsible for fulfilling the covenant.

Instead of Israel's election affording immunity from God's judgment, it formed the basis for that judgment. "Therefore" joins covenant election and punishment in an inseparable sequence. "I will punish" means "visit" with the specific purpose of examination of performance. A literal translation reveals that Israel's performance was deserving of punishment: "I will visit upon you all your iniquities" (3:2*b*). "Iniquities" means perversity of behavior. Examples may be found everywhere in the Book of Amos.

The questioning style of 3:3-8 marks this passage as a separate unit from 3:1-2. The effect Amos' audience saw was a prophet preaching. The cause behind the effect was God's call.

Amos sought to persuade his audience that he was an authentic messenger of God (vv. 3-8). His first illustration was a common observation. Two people walking together (the effect) meant that they had "made an appointment" (the cause). They agreed to walk together.

The next four questions come in pairs: the roar of the lion and the voice of the young lion (effects) mean in each case that the prey has already been taken (cause, v. 4); a bird falling to the earth and a snare springing up (effects) mean respectively that a trap had been set and an animal (perhaps a bird) had been captured (causes, v. 5); a trumpet blast (cause) and evil (effect) mean respectively that people will fear (effect) and God has acted (cause, v. 6).

Verse 7 represents a lapse in the series of questions. It is a statement of principle aimed at authenticating the prophet's ministry. The principle involved here is that God reveals his plans to his prophets before he carries them out.

If the lion roars (the cause), fear (the effect) is inevitable. If the Lord speaks (the cause), a person will prophesy (the effect). With the lion's roar motif (1:2; 3:4), Amos explained his presence before his audience preaching God's word.

The messages of judgment are against Samaria, the political capital (vv. 9-12); Bethel, the religious center (vv. 13-14); and the many houses of the rich, their status symbols (v. 15). A general audience from Samaria seems to be the persons addressed. The use of direct address, "your defenses" and "your strongholds," is the evidence for this identification of hearers (v. 11).

The prophet's imperatives (v. 9) are designed to capture the attention of his audience. He wanted his hearers to think about what it would be like to have those who were experts in terror tactics and oppression to observe them. "Proclaim" is literally "cause to be heard." "Strongholds" were storehouses for treasures obtained through violence and oppression. These structures served also as part of a city's defense system.

Representatives from foreign powers were commanded to observe "the great tumults" (boundless terrors) and "the oppressions" (extortions) in the midst of Samaria. The implication is that the observers would be shocked.

The primary indictment against the citizens of Samaria is that "they do not know how to do right" (v. 10). "Right" means that which is in front, straight, upright, honest, or just. That the indictment is aimed at the rich is made clear by the verb translated "those who store up." It was the rich who amassed treasures from acts of "violence" against people and "robbery" (devastation) of material goods.

Amos's "therefore" reaches back to the indictment (v. 10) as the basis for Yahweh's judgment (v. 11). "An adversary" would plunder the very "strongholds" where Israel's plundered treasures had been stored. "Surround the land" implies that the entire nation would be affected by the judgment.

Amos knew that a shepherd was required to produce evidence for the owner in the form of fragments from the animal attacked by a lion (Ex. 22:13). "Rescues" means "snatches," or "delivers." "Two legs," or "a piece of an ear" would not be much evidence, but either would be adequate to demonstrate the nature of the loss. Similarly "the corner of a couch" and "part of a bed" would not be much evidence of the comfortable life Samaria's citizens had enjoyed. But even fragments would serve as evidence that a predator had ravaged God's flock. Bits and pieces would testify to Samaria's fall, but would hardly serve as a basis for hope.

The word "house" ties the remaining three verses together: "house of Jacob" (v. 13), "Bethel" (house of God, v. 14), and "houses" of the wealthy (v. 15). Politics, religion, and life-style are all condemned. Unnamed witnesses are called upon to hear and to attest to Yahweh's punishment of Israel (v. 13). God has been known to them as "the God of hosts" in holy wars against their enemies. But now "Israel" is the nation to be punished.

"The day" of God's visitation would be for the purpose of punishing Israel for "his transgressions" (v. 14). Israel's rebellions were associated with religious life at the royal shrine in Bethel. To cut off the horns of the altar would deny asylum to the fugitive. Israel's rebellions were so acute that Yahweh pledged to destroy the place of refuge. Destruction of the altars would leave the nation devoid of its means of atonement.

The comfortable life-style of the rich in Samaria was symbolized by their extravagance in housing. "Winter house" and "summer house" probably designate the luxury of two separate dwellings (compare 1 Kings 21:1,18). "Houses of ivory" were dwellings lavishly decorated with ivory. The phrase translated "the great houses" may refer to the amassing of real estate by the rich, or to the many (not great) houses bought or confiscated by the wealthy. In the judgment God vowed to "smite," consign to "perish," and bring to "an end" all such activity.

Prepare to Meet Your God (4:1-13)

Impending judgment is the theme of chapter 4 (v. 12). "Prepare to meet your God" means get braced for God's judgment. Amos indicted the women of Samaria (4:1-3), condemned worship at two major shrines (4:4-5), illustrated God's patience in dealing with

Israel's steadfast rebellion (4:6-11), and announced judgment upon
the nation (v. 12). The final verse is the first of three doxologies in
the book (compare 5:8-9 and 9:5-6). Either the streets or the
marketplace in Samaria is the setting for this oracle.

The "cows of Bashan" (v. 1) were the elite, luxury-loving wives of
wealthy court officials. They did not "oppress the poor" or "crush
the needy" in overt acts against them. But they did pressure their
"husbands" to "bring" more and more to satisfy their self-indulgent
appetites. The reference to "drink" may suggest that alcoholism was
a problem among Samaria's pampered darlings. Of primary concern
to the prophet here was not the indulgence of the women in
"drink," but the consequences suffered by the poor as a result of
their demands upon their husbands. The series of three participles
to describe what these women were doing stresses their dogged
determination to get their way whatever the cost to somebody else.
They went on oppressing the poor, crushing the needy, and nagging
their husbands.

God's judgment upon such women is announced in the form of an
oath (vv. 2-3). When God speaks, his word is serious and certain.
But when he binds what he says by taking an oath, it is even more
serious and certain. For God to swear by "his holiness" is for him to
swear by himself and to assert the absolutely irrevocable nature of
the oath taken. "Days are coming upon you" is eschatological
(relating to the end time) language (v. 2*b*). The future "days" for the
"cows of Bashan" would be dark days of judgment.

The verb translated "they shall take . . . away" is used typically to
describe deportation. With "hooks" and "fishhooks" corpses would
be dragged out of the city, or captives would be fastened together. A
common practice was to run a hook through the lip of each captive
and then attach a rope to the hook to bind the captives together. An
additional indignity may be implied by the next line. The word
translated "the last of you" may be rendered "the afterwards of you."
Each captive would be hooked in the lip and in the posterior in a
most humiliating fashion.

Samaria's dainty darlings would be dragged or led through walls
breached so many times no one would bother to look for a gate (v. 3).
Where the corpses or captives would be "cast forth" is not clear.
"Harmon" seems to be a place name, but its location is unknown.
Some interpreters think the text should read "Hermon." Hermon is

located in the Bashan range. "Cows of Bashan" would be cast forth into Bashan.

The second oracle in chapter 4 concerns Bethel, the king's sanctuary, and Gilgal, another significant shrine in Israel since the days of entry into the land. The imperative verb translated "come" is the word normally used by priests to urge pilgrims to enter a sanctuary to worship (v. 4). "Bethel" was one of the two state shrines Jeroboam I established as an alternate to Jerusalem when the northern tribes broke away from Judah (1 Kings 12:28-32). "Transgress," a second plural imperative, was the exact opposite of what pilgrims expected to hear. This word describes rebellion, a break with Yahweh. They thought their activity at the shrine would establish community with God. "Gilgal" was established as a memorial to God's miraculous help when they entered the Promised Land (Josh. 4:19-24). But Amos termed what pilgrims did there an intensification of "transgression." "Multiply" is the third plural imperative Amos used to instruct pilgrims.

The prophet's fourth plural imperative, "Bring," is a causative form of the same verb translated "come" at the beginning of verse 4. A normal religious experience for a pilgrim involved the presentation of "sacrifices," "tithes," "a sacrifice of thanksgiving," and "freewill offerings."

The word rendered "sacrifices" designates any offering in which an animal was slain (v. 4). "Tithes" represented 10 percent of the pilgrims' harvests of grain, wine, and oil, as well as the increase in their herds and flocks (Deut. 12:17; 14:23). "Offer a sacrifice" means kindle or burn an offering (v. 5). The fact that what was to be offered was from "that which is leavened" implies a thank offering (Lev. 7:13). Inclusion of the term rendered "thanksgiving" leaves no doubt about the kind of offering under consideration. "Freewill offerings" were voluntary expressions of devotion.

The phrases rendered "every morning" and "every three days" may be related to "multiply transgressions" (v. 4). Bringing such offerings in lavish quantities only intensified their rebellion. Amos urged pilgrims to "proclaim" (call out, or announce) their "freewill offerings." He ordered worshipers to "publish them" (literally, "cause to be heard"). The reason the prophet commanded pilgrims to "proclaim" and "publish" their freewill offerings was that they loved to do it. "*Your* sacrifices," "*your* tithes," and "so *you* love to do" (author's italics) imply that what they did in rituals had nothing to do with Yahweh. The mechanics of religion had become a substitute for their covenant responsibilities, a cloak for their daily acts of oppression against their brothers.

Israel's rebellion expressed through self-serving rituals of worship (vv. 4-5) was but the culmination of her stubborn refusal to repent (vv. 6-11). Yahweh's punitive acts were designed to secure Israel's repentance. But the nation steadfastly refused to return to God.

"Cleanness of teeth" and "lack of bread" describe a famine (v. 6). With emphatic language the Lord claimed responsibility for the famine: "I, even I gave to you cleanness of teeth" (literally). Israel's response to God's act is reported in the last line: "Yet you did not return to me." The form employed in this oracle is repeated in each succeeding oracle, including the closing divine oracle formula. The prophet's meaning is not discerned by viewing the report of each calamity in isolation. Only when the series is heard in its entirety does the staccato effect of the repetition make its impact. These verses function as one indictment against Israel (vv. 6-11). The tension created by the sequence of oracles is resolved in the announcement of judgment in verse 12.

Drought is the calamity reported in verses 7 and 8. Again with emphatic language, the Lord claimed to be the source of this disaster. Weak from thirst, sufferers wandered from city to city in search of water (v. 8). But they were not desperate enough to return to God.

Crop failure caused by plant diseases and locusts is the third plague Yahweh brought upon Israel (v. 9). "Blight" (smut) and "mildew" ruined their "gardens" and "vineyards." "Locusts" ate their "fig trees" and their "olive trees." But the intended response of Israel's repentance was not gained.

Pestilence and war are paired as the fourth plague Yahweh sent upon his people (v. 10). "After the manner of Egypt" refers to the plagues God brought upon the Egyptians to gain the release of Israel from bondage there (Ex. 9:3-7). "Pestilence" always denotes a lethal epidemic. That is why it often stands parallel with "sword." The "young men" made up the nation's best combat troops. "Horses" pulled their war chariots. But God's hand in it all brought death, destruction, and defeat. Even so, stubborn Israel refused to return to God.

The final oracle in the series reports some unnamed divine

intervention in Israel's history (v. 11). God's overthrow of Sodom and Gomorrah became proverbial for the complete destruction of political entities (Isa. 13:19; Jer. 49:18). The words "as a brand plucked out of the burning" may refer to the destruction wrought upon Israel by Syria (2 Kings 13:1-9). Even divine intervention did not turn Israel back to Yahweh.

"Prepare to meet your God" (v. 12) is not the prophet's final call to repentance. It is an alert to get braced for the judgment encounter with God. "Thus" and "this" point forward and backward respectively. But that to which they point is uncertain. Perhaps the awesome reality of an encounter with God is the threatened judgment. "Prepare to meet your God" is ritual language. But it is doubtful that Amos is recommending one more ritual.

The awesome reality of the God Israel must meet in judgment is described in verse 13. This doxology is probably one stanza of a praise hymn. The other two doxologies (5:8-9 and 9:5-6) may be two other stanzas of the same hymn. God is pictured in this stanza (v. 13) as the creator. He is not a hidden God, but one who reveals his "thought" to mankind. He controls nature and manifests himself to man. The one whose name is "the Lord" (Yahweh) and who is "the God of hosts" (leading the hosts of Israel in holy war) is the one Israel must meet in judgment.

Funeral for Israel (5:1-17)

This oracle begins with a messenger's summons to his audience to give heed to his message (v. 1). "This word" is God's word, as the closing messenger formula indicates. The verb translated "take up" is a participle meaning lift up and bear away in most contexts. Here it refers to lifting up a song in mourning. "Over you" might as properly be translated "upon you," "against you," or "concerning you."

Amos announced the death of one whose identity his listeners had not learned. The abruptness of his direct address, "over you," and his insertion of "O house of Israel" in the blank reserved for the name of the deceased must have been shocking. It would be comparable to reading your own name in an obituary column of a newspaper. "House of Israel" means the Northern Kingdom.

Amos spoke earlier of Israel's judgment as a future experience. But in this funeral song he refers to their fall as an accomplished fact

(v. 2). "No more to rise" is literally "not she will cause to add to rise." "Virgin Israel" is the earliest reference to Israel as a woman. The term means both youthfulness and virginity. Israel was young as nations go in Amos' day (about 170 years old), and she was about to come to an untimely end.

Not only had the nation "fallen" in death, but it had been abandoned also (v. 2b). "Forsaken" refers to the corpse stretched out upon the ground and left unattended. It was upon "her land," the land God had given them, that the nation lay dead "with none to raise her up." What a hopeless picture! Verse 3 is clearly an extension of the funeral song in verse 2. It gives the reason for the lament. A military conflagration caused Israel to fall. In such a crisis, each city would send whatever number of men it could muster. To have only 10 percent of the men return is no remnant of hope. That percentage symbolized a nation so decimated as to have no future.

Amos set the exhortation to seek Yahweh and "live" (vv. 4-7) immediately adjacent to his dirge of death (vv. 1-3). In popular understanding, the priest's exhortation "seek me and live" meant to seek Yahweh through the rituals of a sanctuary. For the prophet to exhort Israelites to seek Yahweh and in the same breath forbid them to seek a sanctuary must have been confusing. How could they seek Yahweh if they could not go to the ancient shrines where he had been found in the past? Possibly the prophet was urging his audience to seek Yahweh by seeking a prophet instead of a sanctuary. Amos could have been pointing to himself as he urged Israelites to seek a word from Yahweh. As God's prophet, he had the word of life.

"Bethel" had been revered as a worship site since the days of Israel's ancestor Jacob (Gen. 28:19). It had become the royal shrine in the Northern Kingdom (7:13). "Gilgal" was established as a significant worship center during Israel's conquest of Canaan (Josh. 4:19-24). Its parallel position with "Bethel" here and in 4:4 implies that it maintained popular prestige in the time of Amos. "Beersheba," in Judah, had ancient associations with Isaac (Gen. 26:23) as a place where God manifested himself. Pilgrims from the Northern Kingdom continued to visit that site even after their split with Judah.

A play on words is evident in the Hebrew text (v. 5b). Various proposals have been made in efforts to display the alliteration in the first line and the abrupt contrast in the second line. An example might be instructive: Gilgal will go to the gallows, and Bethel will become pandemonium. The names of both sites are placed in the emphatic position in the sentence. Verb forms in the reference to Gilgal indicate the absolute certainty of the assertion: "Gilgal shall surely go into exile." The term translated "nought" may mean grievous trouble, religious perversion, or idolatry. What a prospect for "Bethel," meaning "house of God"!

The speaker in verse 4 is Yahweh, "Seek me and live." But it is the prophet who exhorts Israel in verse 6 to "seek [Yahweh] and live." This verse interprets verses 4 and 5. "Break out like fire" is a threat of war. Failure to seek the Lord would bring unquenchable "fire" (war) upon Bethel. "House of Joseph" refers to the tribes located in central Palestine (Ephraim and Manasseh), but probably stands for the entire Northern Kingdom. Yahweh, the source of life, would come like an unquenchable fire upon Israel.

The addresses are designated by descriptive participles, "O you who turn" and "cast down" (v. 7). These are the ones who are urged to seek Yahweh. They were turning sweet "justice" to bitter "wormwood" (injustice). They "cast down [discarded] righteousness to the earth" in the process. When the courts of Israel overturned justice, then it was that "righteousness" was discarded as worthless. It was trampled underfoot.

The nature of the God Israel was urged to seek is set forth in a second doxology (vv. 8-9). Here, as in the other two doxologies (4:13; 9:5-6), Yahweh is praised as creator. He "made" the stars, controls "day" and "night," and waters the earth with rain (v. 8). The one who creates and controls the universe (v. 8) has power to judge people (v. 9). People, no matter how "strong," and fortresses, no matter how solid, are no match for God.

The antecedent of "they" (v. 10) may be the greedy rich who used the courts to oppress the poor (compare v. 7). The verb form suggests that their hatred was a settled and determined stance. "Him who reproves" is the advocate of right. He handed down the decision of the elders as to who was in the right. "Him who speaks the truth" is emphatic. The term translated "truth" means the whole truth. Such a witness was needed to establish justice. It is little wonder that greedy rich people abhorred these persons.

Usually "therefore" (v. 11) is a transition word used to shift from indictment to judgment. But an additional word of accusation is inserted before the announcement of judgment here. The rich used the courts to exploit the poor. Their land was confiscated for debts owed. High rent was charged for the use of the land in the form of "exactions of wheat." By such oppressive measures wealthy land-owners had "built houses of hewn stone" and "planted pleasant vineyards." The additional accusation in verse 11 is similar to futility curses outside the Old Testament (v. 11*b*). It is futile to build fine houses and not enjoy living in them, or to plant splendid vineyards but not have the satisfaction of drinking their wine.

Amos may be the speaker in verse 12. The multitude of Israel's "transgressions" and the great number of her "sins" were well known to the prophet. "Transgressions" probably means rebellions associated with their covenant relationship. "Sins" implies their proneness to miss the mark.

Again with participles descriptive of his audience's deeds, the prophet identified the target of this oracle (v. 12*b*). The root meaning of the verb rendered "afflict" is to bind, tie up, restrict. It is the "righteous," those who are innocent and should go free, who are bound by perverted justice. Some in the prophet's audience are accused of taking "a bribe." The verbal root from which "bribe" is derived means "cover." To take a bribe is to accept cover money (hush money) and decide a case based on profit instead of truth. The final accusation continues the charge of corruption of justice. To turn "the needy" aside in "the gate" was to deny justice to them.

"In such a time" is literally "in that time." Perhaps the prophet meant in a future time, a particular future time. That time is characterized as "an evil time." Evil probably means calamitous. What time fits that description any better than Amos' concept of the day of the Lord? A prudent man would keep silent in that day because it would be too late to speak up. The nation would be in exile, and no courts would remain in which to speak.

Once again in this chapter Amos exhorted his audience to "seek." First, it was "seek me and live" (v. 4). Then it was "seek the Lord and live" (v. 6). Now it is "seek good, and not evil, that you may live" (v. 14). "Live" is the result of seeking in each case. But is seeking good the same as seeking God? The two are related. They represent two dimensions of true religion: (1) seeking God, being concerned with God, devoting oneself to God, and (2) seeking good, being concerned with good, devoting oneself to good. The bottom line in true religion is not going to a sanctuary and going through a ritual. It is going to a brother and doing good. Seeking "good" means the development of a relationship with a person in order to do that person good. "Good" as Amos used it is the establishment of justice in the gate, and that comes about when good men "hate evil, and love good" (v. 15).

Amos promised life to those who would "seek good, and not evil." He assured them of the presence of "the Lord, the God of hosts" just as they had been saying. But Amos declared that God's presence with them was not guaranteed by going through religious rituals. Seeking God must manifest itself in hating evil, seeking good, and establishing justice.

"It may be" means "perhaps" (v. 15b). God is sovereign and, thus, the best the prophet could offer to those who would seek good is "perhaps." "Willl be gracious" means the granting of favor and help to those who do not merit them. "Remnant" means remainder, or what is left after God's judgment has fallen. "Joseph" refers here to the Northern Kingdom.

Verses 16 and 17 appear to be a funeral song. Funeral songs, sighs, and sobs would be intoned in the open "squares," the narrow "streets," the farms, and "the vineyards." No facet of life would be untouched. Death and mourning would be everywhere.

And when would those skilled in lamentation (professional mourners) join their voices to the wails and cries of the people to mourn the dead in Israel? It would be when Yahweh passes "through the midst" of Israel. He had passed over Israel and passed through the midst of the Egyptians earlier, leaving death in every Egyptian household. Now his coming would mean death to Israel.

What Does the Lord Require? (5:18-27)

The first reference to "the day of the Lord" in the Old Testament is found in Amos. But it is doubtful that he coined the expression. As a matter of fact, the prophet was clearly grappling with his audience's understanding of what "the day of the Lord" would mean to them. They had to know about it to "desire" it.

This is the first of two woe-cries in the Book of Amos (5:18; 6:1). In the prophet's first recorded use of the form, he took a creative step which no one before him had taken. He related the popular yearning for "the day of the Lord" to funerary lamentation. Israel thought the day would bring light (life). Amos said it would be a day of darkness (death). The prophet's woe-cry for those who "desire" the day of the Lord reveals his understanding of what that day would mean to Israel. To cry "woe" was to lament over them as though they were already dead.

The prophet's question "Why would you have the day of the Lord?" is literally, "Why this for you the day of the Lord?" He proceeded to clarify what the day would mean by a terse assertion, "It is darkness, and not light" (v. 18c). "Darkness" symbolizes evil, calamity, and destruction. "Light" symbolizes good, salvation, peace, and life. Israel understood correctly that "darkness" applied to God's enemies and "light" to his friends. Their problem was the identification of the enemies and the friends. For Amos, those who pervert justice and oppress the poor could not possibly be the friends of God.

Amos illustrated what the day of the Lord would mean to Israel by a comparison (v. 19). His "man" stands for the nation. The man escaped from the lion only to meet a bear. He escaped from the bear by entering the safety of a house, only to die from the bite of a serpent. The fatal bite came when the man felt himself to be secure. Israel felt secure. But the day of the Lord would be a day of death. Amos wanted Israel to admit that the day of the Lord would be a day of "darkness" for them (v. 20).

The shift to first-person speech in verse 21 separates this oracle (vv. 21-27) from the one preceding it. Amos probably preached this oracle at Bethel. It is an evaluation of Israel's worship (vv. 21-23), an exhortation to practice justice (v. 24), and a threat of exile for those who rely on sacrifices and worship pagan gods (vv. 25-27).

The theme of verses 21-23 is God's total rejection of every aspect of Israel's worship. Nowhere else in the Old Testament are these two harsh words of rejection set one after the other (v. 21). "Hate" is the stronger of the two. It describes all the resources of a person set against someone or something. "Despise" means "reject." Israel's "feasts" are the object of God's rejection.

Israel's festal "assemblies" brought no pleasure to God (v. 21b). "Burnt offerings" (v. 22a) are "going up offerings," a name derived from the rise of the smoke from the altar where the whole animal was burned. The term translated "cereal offerings" designates all sorts of sacrifices in Amos' usage. "Accept" is the word the priest used to express official approval of sacrifices. Amos used the term with a negative particle to announce Yahweh's rejection of Israel's sacrificial offerings.

Part of the peace offering was burnt on the altar (v. 22b). The rest was eaten by the worshipers. It symbolized a shared meal between God and his people in which the wholeness of their relationship was reestablished. "I will . . . look upon" is from a term that usually refers to watching or paying attention to people (Ps. 33:13). Amos used a negative particle with it to mean that God would pay no attention to the ritual activity symbolizing renewal of a vital relationship to him.

"Take away" means literally "cause to turn aside" (v. 23). "From me" is more precisely, "from upon me," as though the noise of Israel's songs was a burden for God to bear. The term rendered "noise" is used to describe the din of battle (Joel 3:14). "To the melody of your harps I will not listen" is literally "and the playing of your harps I will not hear." God's rejection is registered dramatically by picturing the deity with shut nostrils (v. 21), closed eyes (v. 22), and stopped-up ears (v. 23). Instead of ritual noises, God wanted to hear the sweet music of "justice" and "righteousness" rolling down "like waters" and an "everflowing stream" (v. 24). Justice and righteousness should roll along with the swell and the force of floods after winter rains and persist unimpeded like a river that never runs dry. Righteousness, not ritual, is what the Lord requires.

Amos held the view, espoused later by Hosea and Jeremiah, that the wilderness era was a time of Israel's complete faithfulness to Yahweh. The expected answer to the rhetorical question in verse 25 is No. "Sacrifices" and "offerings" were not brought to God in the wilderness. Why they were not has been the subject of debate among scholars for a long time. Was it because they were not required, or was it because the resources for them were lacking? Some interpreters have argued that sacrifices were never a legitimate part of Israel's worship (compare Jer. 7:21-22). Others favor the lack of opportunity and resources to fulfill the requirements as the correct explanation. The meaning of the oracle in this case would be that Israel maintained a close relationship to God without the benefit of sacrifice.

Verse 26 is a continuation of the rhetorical question begun in verse 25, not a threat that Israel would be forced to worship astral deities in exile. Israel did not worship pagan gods in the wilderness. That practice developed after they entered the land of Canaan. "Exile beyond Damascus" is the threatened judgment for worshiping homemade gods (v. 27).

We're Number One (6:1-7)

The prophet's second woe-saying was aimed at the rich, powerful, ruling class. He condemned them for bragging about wealth amassed through violence (vv. 1-3) and for lounging in luxury while the rest of the nation was breaking under the burden of poverty (vv. 4-6). But Amos announced a judgment suitable for such arrogant, uncaring rulers (v. 7).

Amos used participles to describe the conduct of his audience. "At ease" probably means secure, confident, carefree. "Zion" stands for Judah, the Southern Kingdom. "Those who feel secure" is literally "the ones trusting." "Mountain of Samaria" may have religious and military implications respectively. These were false sources of security from the prophet's viewpoint.

The irony in the label (v. 1b) Amos gave the braggarts who led the Northern Kingdom is not visible until God's judgment upon them is announced (v. 7). "The notable men" comes from a word that means "pierce." It designates "marked men," men of distinction. In their own estimation they were the preeminent rulers of the number one nation in the world, a highly inflated opinion to say the least. The upper class had gained control of the nation through devious means. This forced the poor into subjection and dependence upon them for everything.

Verse 2 has been interpreted in two basic ways: (1) as a warning from Amos to the leaders of Israel that their cities would fall just as others had; or (2) as the prophet's quotation of words from Israel's leaders bragging on their greatness. The latter method of handling the text seems best. In a comparison with "Calneh," "Hamath," or "Gath" Israel would stand out as superior. This is simply proud boasting on the part of Israel's "notable men."

Amos charged these proud boasters with postponement of a day of reckoning for their arrogant attitudes and persistent violence (v. 3). To "put far away" is to banish any thought that a day of "evil" awaited them. "Evil day" means day of calamity, a time of destructive judgment. "Seat of violence" designates the throne or judicial seat used by these rulers to bring a day of calamity upon the poor. Such actions hastened their own day of disaster.

The participles in verses 4-6 describe additional actions calling for the downfall of the prophet's audience. The woe-cry is not repeated in verse 4, as the Revised Standard Version translation implies, but the woe-saying extends through verse 6. A carefree life of eating, drinking, and making merry is portrayed here. The "beds of ivory" on which they lounged were inlaid with ivory designs. "Stretch themselves" means sprawled, or draped as in a drunken stupor. Choice cuts of "lambs" and "calves" formed the foundation of their diet. The word rendered "stall" means fattening pen.

"Sing idle songs" means improvise in the sense of singing extemporaneously, or wail (screech) in meaningless sounds (v. 5). "To the sound of the harp" suggests that their efforts at singing were accompanied by stringed instruments. Perhaps the mention of "David" means that these revelers imagined their musical skills were comparable to those of David. By a slight change in the alignment of the Hebrew letters, a different interpretation has been proposed. It is that those stuffed with food and drunk with wine took their jugs and fists as instruments and thought they made delightful music with them.

The "bowls" from which these celebrants drank wine (v. 6) are mentioned elsewhere only in connection with rituals of worship. These wide-mouthed basins were used to splash the blood of sacrificial animals against the altar (Ex. 24:6). Their use here exposes the intemperance of the prophet's audience. Only "the finest oils" (first-grade oils) would satisfy the prominent menbers of Israel's society. The word "anoint" may suggest self-appointed status and authority. More likely it refers to cosmetic rubbing of these oils. Their concerns were skin care and erotic aroma.

The sin of such carefree, self-indulgent revelry is revealed in verse 6b. "Joseph" stands for the Northern Kingdom of Israel. The "ruin" (breakdown) of the nation brought no grief to the number one rulers of the number one nation. They were too caught up in the celebration of their own good fortune even to notice the "ruin" of the nation. What an indictment!

Israel's self-acclaimed number one rulers were first in leadership (vv. 1-3) and first in luxury (vv. 4-6). Now with the prophet's "therefore" he points them to the head of the line of captives so that they may be the first to leave it all. The noise of "revelry" (screech, shout) made by those whose custom it had been to "stretch themselves" (sprawl) in drunken stupor would "pass away." By implication the whole nation would suffer the humiliation of exile.

Judgment upon a Prideful Nation (6:8-14)

The judgment of God upon a self-indulgent and uncaring leadership is announced in verse 7. How that judgment would come is explained in verses 8-14. With the oath formula the Lord binds himself to carry out that judgment (v. 8). What God bound himself to do was to "deliver up the city and all that is in it." No doubt "the city" is Samaria. And the grounds for such a harsh judgment are "the pride of Jacob" and "his strongholds."

"Hate" and "abhor" expressed human attitudes in 5:10, but they represent the attitude of Yahweh here (v. 8). What the Lord abhors is "the pride of Jacob," their national self-confidence. The object of God's hatred was Jacob's "strongholds." These "strongholds" were elevated and fortified structures used to stash their treasures taken by violence and to defend their cities in times of military crises. The verb translated "I will deliver up" means abandon. "The city" designates Samaria, the focus of their national optimism. "All that is in it" is literally "her fullness." Likely both the populace and their treasures in the strongholds are covered by this term.

The only prospect offered to survivors of some unnamed disaster is to "die" (v. 9). For ten men to remain in "one house" would seem to be too large a number for a private residence. "House" may mean the king's house. Some contagious pestilence must have been the cause of death, based on the references to burning, the disposal of corpses, and the caution exercised. Answers to several questions in verse 10 remain uncertain. Were there two kinsmen who came to dispose of the bodies? Was the person in the "innermost parts of the house" a survivor or an assistant kinsman? Why was caution to be exercised about mentioning the name of the Lord? It is possible that the conversation is between a kinsman and a lone survivor, as the Revised Standard Version translation implies. However, the term translated "he who burns him" may be a second kinsman. The word rendered "kinsman" refers to a relative on the father's side of the family. If "he who burns him" is correctly identified as a second kinsman, this one is a relative on the mother's side of the family.

Verse 9 implies that no one of the ten remaining men survived. Thus, when the voice responded from the innermost parts of the house about survivors, it was probably the second kinsman who answered. The word translated "the man's kinsman" is joined to the next word, rendered "he who burns him," by a conjunction. This would rule out an appositive relationship and suggest that the second word is parallel to the first, each referring to a kinsman. But why did one kinsman caution the other about mentioning the name of the Lord? The reason for caution is that to "mention" (remember, memorialize) the name of the Lord in lamentation or prayer would risk God's appearance to renew the death-causing pestilence.

The Lord's destruction of "the great house" and "the little house" means that all segments of Israel's society would feel God's blow in judgment (v. 11). With the questions in verse 12 the prophet provokes his audience to consider how absurd their actions are with regard to "justice" and "righteousness." It is insane to pervert justice so that it becomes a poison to kill rather than a balm to heal. "The fruit of righteousness" means the benefits of living by the authoritative norms. It is ridiculous when expected benefits are turned to "wormwood" (bitterness) by the perversion of the courts.

Israel's boasting in her own accomplishments (v. 13) is countered by the announcement of God's judgment against them (v. 14). An ironic twist may be intended by the way "Lo-debar" is spelled in the Hebrew text. Their rejoicing in Lo-debar is rejoicing in "nothing" (literally). "Karnaim" is a dual form of the word for "horn," a symbol of strength. By their own strength these Israelite conquerors took strength (power, authority) for themselves. The name of the place provoked their proud boast.

Notice that it is God who threatens to "raise up . . . a nation" against "the house of Israel" (v. 14). Though the "nation" is not named, its intent is clear. They would come to conquer the conquerors. "Hamath" marked the northern limits of Israel and the "brook of the Arabah" designated the southern limits. Every segment of the land would feel the squeeze of the foe's oppression. That is Amos' final word in the words-of-Amos section of the book.

The Visions of Amos
7:1 to 9:15

Chapters 7 through 9 contain five vision-reports in autobiographical style, a biographical account of Amos' encounter with Amaziah, and a variety of sayings. Four of the five vision-reports follow a set pattern: an introductory formula, the vision-content, and a dialogue between Amos and Yahweh. The fifth vision-report departs from the pattern altogether. In the first two Amos saw an event; he watched the event move toward completion; he interceded for Israel; and the Lord revoked his decision.

In the next two vision-reports Amos was shown objects whose meaning was not obvious; the Lord gave an interpretation of the vision; Amos accepted the Lord's decree and did not intercede for Israel. The prophet initiated the dialogue in the first two vision-reports. Yahweh initiated conversation following the next two. The first, second, and fourth vision-reports are introduced with the same words: "Thus the Lord God showed me." A shortened form, "He showed me," is used in the third. But the final one begins with the direct statement, "I saw the Lord" (9:1).

Visions of Judgment (7:1-9)

"Showed me" is actually "caused me to see" (v. 1). The participle translated "was forming" implies that God was the one who formed the locusts. "Behold" focuses attention upon the time of the forming locust swarm, "the beginning of the shooting up of the latter growth." The time is just after the spring rains which caused the final growth of grass. A locust plague then would be completely devastating since there would be no more rain until the next year. "After the king's mowings" pinpoints the time more specifically. This phrase probably means that the king had the right to the first cutting of the grass as a tax to feed his cavalry (1 Kings 18:5). If the second growth were to be lost to the locusts, nothing would be left for the people.

Amos watched the swarm of locusts devour all the "grass" of the land (v. 2). He understood the implications for Israel and proceeded to plead for forgiveness. His cry, "O Lord God," is language appropriate to prayer. It expresses both the exaltation of God and his close relationship to Amos. The prophet's appeal for God to "forgive" the people means that he recognized the locust plague as punishment. It is worth observing that a significant part of a prophet's function was intercessory prayer. "How can Jacob stand?" is a question concerned with Israel's survival (v. 2). The nation's helplessness is pictured in the statement, "He is so small." Amos did not believe Israel could survive the coming devastation revealed through the vision.

"The Lord repented" does not suggest that the Lord had sinned and turned away from it (v. 3). It means that he changed his mind, prompted by deep emotion. With a sigh of relief, Yahweh turned away (at least momentarily) from the earlier decision to destroy Israel. Based on the intercession of Amos, the Lord announced that he would not carry out the locust plague.

The second vision is like the first in form and meaning. Only the instrument of judgment and the content of the intercession are different. "Fire" may refer to war or drought. Here the latter is more likely. Amos watched the fire devour "the great deep" and "the land." Severe drought would dry up the streams and burn up the vegetation. "The great deep" was the source of springs and rivers and "the land" refers either to the territory of Israel (Mic. 2:4) or to the nation as God's special portion (Deut. 32:9). Again as in the first vision, Amos perceived that Israel could not survive the destruction revealed through the vision.

The prophet's prayer is for God to "cease" (v. 5), not "forgive" (v. 2). "Cease" means stop. Amos asked God to stop the judgment by fire. He based the petition on his assessment that "Jacob" was too small to survive the announced destruction. Again the Lord "repented" and with emphatic language promised, "This also shall not be" (v. 6).

The third vision has a shortened introductory formula, "He showed me" (v. 7). What Yahweh caused the prophet to see first of all was "the Lord." He stood by a wall "built with a plumb line." The implication is that the wall had been erected properly. The plumb line in the Lord's hand meant that the wall was about to be checked to determine whether or not it was still plumb.

This time the Lord initiated conversation with Amos. First, he asked Amos to identify what he saw (v. 8a). Apparently what the prophet saw, a "plumb line," was exactly what the Lord hoped he would see. With such a tool, a builder could erect a straight wall or check the straightness of a wall.

The Lord explained the vision to Amos, lest he misunderstand its meaning (v. 8b). It was the Lord himself who was "setting a plumb line." "My people" refers to God's covenant partner. Thus, God was checking his own people to see if they had remained true to the covenant. The threat, "I will never again pass by them," means that

God found Israel to be out of plumb. Twice already the Lord had "passed by" Israel because of the prophet's intercession. But "never again" would he do so.

The Lord's decree of judgment is an interpretation of the vision (v. 9). Israel's religion and her government failed to stand the test of straightness. All of Israel's religious sites are included in the two designations, "high places" and "sanctuaries." "Isaac" is an alternate name for the Northern Kingdom, as the following parallel line makes clear. "Shall be made desolate" means the destruction of provisions, as well as depopulation. "Shall be laid waste" means devastated by enemy invasion and deportation.

The final threat is that the Lord "will rise against the house of Jeroboam" (v. 9c). Only the Lord is named as Israel's foe. "With the sword" indicates the instrument of destruction. "The house of Jeroboam" designates the royal house. Judgment would begin at the house of God, and include the house of the king.

Prophet and Priest (7:10-17)

Someone other than Amos narrated the encounter between Amos and Amaziah at Bethel. It reads like an eyewitness account. Three scenes make up this biographical narrative: the priest's report to the king (vv. 10-11), the priest's order to the prophet (vv. 12-13), and the prophet's response to the priest (vv. 14-17). This biographical prophecy is sandwiched between the third and fourth visions because of the threat to the king in verse 9.

Perhaps Amaziah heard Amos give the first three vision-reports. He recognized a threat to the kingdom and to King Jeroboam II as well. Likely Amaziah owed his appointment as "priest of Bethel" to Jeroboam II. For that reason, he felt constrained to send a runner to Jeroboam twenty-five miles away in Samaria to report anything that seemed to threaten the king.

Evidence is lacking that Amos "conspired" with anyone against Jeroboam (v. 10). But both the priest and the king must have known from their own history of dynasties being destroyed or established by the word of a prophet. Amaziah's charge that "the land is not able to bear all his words" implies that the priest had heard the prophet preach a number of times. "Not able to bear" may mean "not able to endure," or "not able to contain." Either rendering suggests that an intolerable level had been reached.

Amaziah gave Jeroboam an excerpt from one of Amos's sermons (v. 11). It purports to be a direct quote, though he did not say specifically that Jeroboam would die by the sword. However, to rise "against the house of Jeroboam" (v. 9) would be to rise against the king personally. Amos had preached in Samaria that Israel would go into "exile" (5:5,27; 6:7). No doubt he preached the same sermon in Bethel. Nothing in the text suggests that the priest examined the truth of the prophet's message. Amos represented a problem and a disturbance to the priest, the people, and the king. Out of loyalty to Jeroboam, Amaziah felt duty-bound to report what Amos was saying.

After reporting Amos to the king, Amaziah ordered the prophet to return to Judah and "never again prophesy at Bethel" (v. 12). The priest must have felt that he had complete authority in Bethel. He made no reference to royal backing as he commanded Amos to return to Judah.

Amaziah called Amos a "seer." Did he mean "visionary" in a derogatory sense? Or was it a title of respect recognizing the charismatic gift of the prophet? Was Amaziah trying to get Amos out of Bethel to get rid of a problem? Or was the priest trying to save the prophet's neck? "Go" and "flee" are imperatives, suggesting the priest's sense of urgency. Emphasis falls upon "there" meaning Judah. Amaziah did not order Amos to stop preaching, nor to quit prophesying against the king. But he did try to direct where he should prophesy. Judah would be a fine place to make a living prophesying. But Bethel was off limits to Amos so far as Amaziah was concerned.

Bethel was "the king's sanctuary" and "the temple of the kingdom" (v. 13), the royal shrine for the Northern Kingdom. The priest recognized the authority of Jeroboam in Bethel and the right of Amos to prophesy. But it is ironic that at Bethel, which means "house of God," the prophet of God and the message of God could not be tolerated.

The question of authority pushes its way into nearly every line of the narrative. Amaziah had authority at Bethel, but he owed allegiance to the king and to God. Jeroboam had authority in Israel and, thus, at Bethel, but he owed allegiance to God. Amos had no official authority at Bethel or in Israel (being from Judah), but he owed allegiance to God. Obviously God's authority should have prevailed when the conflict came. But Amaziah had his job to think

about. Jeroboam was concerned for his kingdom. Amos had his neck
to think about, but he thought more of being faithful to deliver
God's message to Israel.

What did Amos mean by his answer to Amaziah (v. 14)? Did he
deny that he was a prophet? Or did he say that he had not been a
prophet until God took him from following the flock? Should the
verbs be present tense or past tense? Verse 14 has no verb in
Hebrew. A general rule is, when a sentence has no verbs, to make
the verbs of that sentence agree with the tense of the verbs in the
context. "[He] took me" in verse 15 would suggest past tense for the
verbs in verse 14. With past tense verbs Amos would be denying
any association with the professional prophets in Israel or Judah.

Amaziah and Jeroboam knew about prophets attached to shrines
and the king's court. These had the official function of prophesying
disaster for Israel's enemies and peace and prosperity for Israel.
Amos denied any connection with such prophets (v. 14a). He
claimed a dual profession, "herdsman" and "dresser of sycamore
trees" (v. 14b). God took him "from following the flock [sheep]"
(v. 15). "A dresser of sycamore trees" was a person whose job
probably was to puncture the fig-like fruit to make it sweeten. As a
layman, Amos had no connection with a prophetic guild.

Amos explained to Amaziah that his authority for prophesying was
Yahweh's call (v. 15). God "took" him from following the flock and
commissioned him to "go" and "prophesy" to God's people "Israel."
For Amos the basic question was not what to preach nor where to
preach. The sole issue was God's call. Both Amaziah and Jeroboam
thought of the people of Israel as their people. Amos set the record
straight. Israel was God's people. That theological definition placed
the king and the priest under God's jurisdiction. The highest
authority in Israel was God, not the priest at Bethel nor the king in
Samaria.

The only oracle in the Book of Amos against an individual is this
message against Amaziah (vv. 16-17). It begins with the call to
attentiveness (v. 16a). The summons to hear is followed by the
indictment against Amaziah (v. 16bc). By use of the messenger
formula (v. 17a), the punishment is introduced (v. 17bc).

Having settled the question of authority, Amos proceeded to
deliver the message of God to Amaziah (v. 16). The essential
indictment against the priest was that he had commanded Amos not
to prophesy against Israel. But that was precisely what God had

commissioned the prophet to do (v. 15). "Prophesy" and "preach" are parallel, as are "Israel" and "the house of Isaac." The verb translated "preach" literally means "drop." It pictures an impassioned discourse with saliva flowing freely from the mouth of the speaker.

"Therefore" followed by the messenger formula introduces the verdict against the priest (v. 17). He and his family would suffer the same judgment as the rest of the nation. His wife, his children, his land, and he himself would be affected adversely by a foreign invasion. His wife would be forced into harlotry. His children would die by the sword. His land (or country) would be parceled out to the conquerors. And he would die in an "unclean land," a land where Yahweh was not worshiped. The final threat of exile (v. 17) is a word-for-word repetition of Amaziah's report to Jeroboam on the prophet's message (v. 11). All Israel would "surely go into exile." Amaziah had no future because Israel had no future.

Prophecy of the End (8:1-8)

The primary difference between the third and the fourth vision-reports is the symbolic object. It was "a plumb line" in the third vision-report (7:7-9). It is "a basket of summer fruit" here (v. 1). "Summer fruit" is "ripened fruit." A basket of ripened fruit signaled the end of the growing season. At that time, Israelites anticipated divine renewal in harmony with the change of seasons.

The Lord's interpretation denied the hope of renewal (v. 2). The word play is hidden by the translation into English. "Summer" and "end" have similar sounds in Hebrew. Instead of the end of the harvest season signaling the hope of renewal, it symbolized the end of Israel. "The end" accents the finality of the threat repeated from the third vision-report: "I will never again pass by them."

A brief description of "the end" for Israel is given in verse 3. "Wailings" (howlings) in lamentation would replace songs of joy and hope in Yahweh. Their songs of lamentation would be caused by the multitude of scattered corpses and the shame of not being buried. "In that day" points ahead to the day of the Lord referred to in 5:18-20. The word translated "silence" is the same term rendered "hush" in 6:10.

The oracles following the fourth vision-report interpret the message of that report. Mourning over the end of Israel as a nation is the theme of the message. Amos wanted his audience to "hear" the words of their indictment (vv. 4-6) and judgment (vv. 7-8). Those indicted are the greedy merchants who "trample upon [grind, Septuagint] the needy [unmet desires]" and "bring the poor of the land to an end" (v. 4). How they did that is explained in verses 5 and 6.

Amos frequently used the words of his opponents to condemn them. The question in verses 5 and 6 is such a quotation. These merchants observed the holy days but could hardly wait for them to end so that they could get back to their buying and selling. "New moon" was celebrated once every four weeks on the first day of the lunar month. The "sabbath" was observed every seventh day. "Grain" and "wheat" designate marketable cereals. "Offer" is from a verb that means literally to "open." A merchant offered wheat for sale by opening the sack in which it was contained.

The driving motivation in the eagerness of these merchants to do business is epitomized in the phrase "and deal deceitfully." The "ephah" was used to measure the grain as it was sold. It was made "small" in order to cheat the buyer with a short measure of grain. The "shekel" was a weight to measure the silver a buyer used in purchasing the grain. It was made "great" in order to make the buyer give an overweight of silver. A third method of cheating the customer was the use of "false balances." The merchants would bend out of shape the crossbeam of such a balance. Greedy merchants are indicted also for purchasing the poor. They even resorted to the sorry practice of selling the trash left after winnowing the grain.

The judgment is stated in the form of a vow (v. 7) and a question (v. 8). Yahweh's vow that he will "never forget any of their deeds" implies that each one will have his attention in the coming judgment. The answer to the rhetorical question in verse 8 is Yes. "The land" must refer to Israel. "Tremble" describes the shaking of the land by an earthquake. "On this account" points back to the deceitful practices of the greedy merchants and God's avowed judgment.

Days of Final Judgment (8:9-14)

The oracles in verses 9-14 continue to interpret the message of the fourth vision (vv. 1-3). "On that day" is eschatological (v. 9). It refers to "end" time for Israel. It is another of several pointers toward "the day of the Lord" (5:18-20). "I will make the sun go down at noon" refers to an eclipse of the sun. Such an eclipse would have been visible in Israel June 15, 763 BC.

The day of the Lord is described in verse 10 as a day of "mourning." Israel's "feasts" were marked with shouts and songs of joy. But these festivals would be turned into "mourning" and "lamentation." "Sackcloth" and "baldness" were outward signs of mourning. The intensity of that mourning would be like the "mourning for an only son." When an only son died, that meant the end of the family. The "end" of such mourning was as bitter as its beginning.

"The days are coming" points to the day of the Lord (v. 11). The threatened judgment is a "famine," but it is no ordinary famine. It would not be characterized by the lack of "bread" and "water." It would be a famine of "hearing the words of the Lord." Those who refused to hear the word of God would lose the privilege of hearing as their punishment.

In distress, Israel would "seek the word of the Lord" (v. 12). "From sea to sea" probably means all over the earth. "From north to east" likely designates those areas where God's people had been scattered. But no matter how far the seekers might range, their search would end in futility: "they shall not find it." "In that day" (v. 13) renews the emphasis on the coming of the "day of the Lord" upon Israel. "Fair virgins" and "young men" represent the strongest people in the land. They would be the last to grow faint from thirst.

Serious problems confront the interpreter in verse 14. Who were the people described as "those who swear"? Were they the fair virgins and the young men? those wandering from sea to sea? the greedy merchants? And by what gods did they swear? Whoever they were, they worshiped false gods. Their judgment would be to "fall, and never rise again" (v. 14).

No Hiding Place (9:1-6)

Yahweh did not cause the prophet to see in this final vision (9:1-4). It is Yahweh who is seen. Where the Lord was standing when Amos saw him seems to be significant. The Revised Standard Version has the Lord standing "beside the altar." The preposition may be translated "beside," "against," "over," or "upon." In "the plumb line" vision-report, the figure who did the checking stood *upon* the wall (7:7). The same verb and preposition are used here in verse 1. Thus, "upon" the altar would seem to be the precise place where Amos saw Yahweh.

"And he said" introduces the Lord's first-person command and threatened judgment. The oracle is a continuation of the vision, not an interpretation. "Smite" is an imperative verb, but who is ordered to smite is not clear. Was it the prophet, angels, an earthquake, or just a rhetorical command? The "capitals" were the caps of columns supporting the roof of the Temple. Supposedly, to smite them would cause the "thresholds to shake" and would bring the building down on "the heads of all the people." Whoever survived that catastrophe would die by "the sword." Total annihilation is clearly portrayed here. A play on words is used in a double affirmation that no one would remain after God's judgment: "not will he flee for them a fleer and not will he escape for them an escapee" (literally).

Though all thought of a remnant is rejected absolutely (v. 1), five possible avenues of escape from the Lord's pursuit are considered and eliminated (vv. 2-4a). This survey of possible hiding places should be compared with Psalm 139:7-12. In the psalm the Lord's benevolent care is the theme. Here the subject is the Lord's judgment.

The five places an Israelite might consider as places of refuge are: Sheol, heaven, the top of Carmel, the bottom of the sea, and captivity. Sheol and heaven represent the lowest and the highest cosmic limits. The top of Carmel and the bottom of the sea represent the highest and the lowest terrestrial limits. Captivity represents territory beyond Israel's borders. But Yahweh's sovereignty reaches into all these regions.

The basis for God's relentless pursuit of Israel was his sovereign decision to bring the nation to an end (v. 4b). Ordinarily a favorable connotation is associated with God's gaze upon his people. But here his eyes set upon Israel would be "for evil and not for good." "Evil" means all that is bad, chaotic, and calamitous. "Good" means all that is positive, benevolent, and fulfilling.

The doxology in verses 5 and 6 follows the announcement of doom here just as the other doxologies follow judgment oracles (4:13; 5:8-9). God's awesome power to create and control the universe is turned into destructive channels so far as Israel is concerned. When

the Lord "touches the earth" in judgment both nature and mankind
are affected. The earth "melts," people "mourn," and the land
"rises" and "sinks." From his throne in the heavens Yahweh controls
the universe (v. 6). It is Yahweh who gives the rain to refresh the
earth. He is in charge of nature and history. "His name" is worthy of
praise.

Judgment and Hope (9:7-15)

Destruction of Israel is the persistent theme of verses 7-10.
Future hope for Israel is the subject of verses 11-15. The expected
answer to the two rhetorical questions in verse 7 is Yes. What the
comparison of Israel with Ethiopia (Cush) does is to deny any kind
of privileged status to Israel. The answer to the second question is
an assertion that Yahweh had not done anything unique for Israel
when he brought them up from Egypt. He had done the same for
two of Israel's most persistent enemies, "the Philistines" and "the
Syrians."

The theme of the Lord's gaze is picked up again in verse 8
(compare v. 4b). "The sinful kingdom" may mean Israel specifically
or every kingdom that is sinful generally. In either case, Israel is the
target of God's particular gaze. And his intent is to "destroy," not
establish (compare 2:9). He destroyed the Amorites to give Canaan
to Israel. Now he would destroy Israel.

The exception clause in verse 8b seems to contradict the previous
threat of destruction. Some interpreters take this as a clear signal
that some hand other than and later than Amos inserted the
exception. It is argued that a Judean editor observed that part of
"the house of Jacob" (Judah) was still standing. Others contend that
all true prophets allowed for an exception. The expression "I will not
utterly destroy" implies survivors. The idea of a remnant may
extend through verses 9 and 10. Israel's exile would be a sifting
process. "All the sinners" of God's people would die, but the grain
(remnant) would be spared. The pebbles (sinners) would be reserved for judgment, even though they loudly acclaimed their
immunity from such "evil."

The two oracles of hope are introduced with the phrases "In that
day" and "the days are coming" respectively. Consistently in Amos
this language points to the day of the Lord. Only here does that day

take on rosy restoration and prosperity. Most interpreters take verses 11 through 15 to be additions to the text of Amos at some time after the fall of Jerusalem in 587 BC. A few interpreters maintain that the oracles of hope are at home in Amos's materials because hope for a remnant is scattered throughout the book.

The first-person address used throughout these oracles marks the promises as divine utterances. God is the one who will "raise up the booth of David" (v. 11), "restore the fortunes" of Israel (v. 14), and "plant them upon their land" (v. 15). "The booth of David that is fallen" (v. 11) is taken to be the split in the kingdom in 931 BC (some date the division in 922 BC) by those who identify the oracle as the message of Amos. Most take it to mean the destroyed city of Jerusalem, with breached walls and burned buildings. "The days of old" in this case would refer to the days before the fall of the city in 587 BC.

In the restoration, Israel would again "possess the remnant of Edom" and all the nations which belonged originally to David's kingdom (v. 12). "Who are called by my name" means those nations that belonged to God. The list would include all the nations dominated by Israel. James quoted this passage in his address to the council at Jerusalem (Acts 15:16-17).

Israel's new day would be characterized by productive crops, restored fortunes, fruitful vineyards and gardens, and secure anchorage in "their land" (vv. 13-15). For "the plowman" to "overtake the reaper" suggests such a productive crop that the harvest would not all be in from one season until it was time to prepare the soil for the next (v. 13). In the days ahead, the process of pressing the juice out of the grapes to make wine would not be completed when sowing time arrived. So abundant would be the harvest that the old promise of a land "which flows with milk and honey" (Num. 14:8) would become a reality with reference to "sweet wine."

"Restore the fortunes" is literally "return the captivity" (v. 14). It describes Yahweh's change from wrath to mercy in his relationship to his people. The context implies a return from exile to rebuild their cities and to replant their vineyards and gardens. Amos had pronounced judgment upon the powerful rich people in Israel who perverted justice to build up their own estates (5:10-11). But they would not enjoy the benefits of owning fine houses and pleasant vineyards. In the coming days they would enjoy their rebuilt houses as well as their vineyards and gardens.

God's promised new day and new relationship would be permanent (v. 15). Again Israel would occupy their land. Never again would they be uprooted. The gift of the land would be reaffirmed. All of these blessings represent the unconditional promise of Israel's God, as the closing messenger formula indicates.

OBADIAH

Introduction

Obadiah is the smallest book in the Old Testament, but the problems of dating and interpreting it are out of all proportion to its size. On the surface it seems to be short and simple. A careful investigation reveals the complexity of this little book.

The Author

Obadiah's name means either "worshiper of Yahweh" or "servant of Yahweh." No references are made in the superscription or in the book to the prophet's family or his date. Internal evidence reveals that Obadiah was probably a Judean who hated Edom and held the view that Yahweh would judge that nation severely. He was familiar with other oracles against the nations which included Edom. A comparison of Obadiah verses 1-5 with Jeremiah 49:9,14-16 indicates one of three possibilities: Obadiah borrowed from Jeremiah, Jeremiah borrowed from Obadiah, or both borrowed from an earlier oracle. The last suggestion seems best.

The Date

The occasion standing behind and prompting Obadiah's prophecy was some destruction of Judah and Jerusalem in which Edom had a part. Several dates have been proposed, but the one that seems most likely is 587 BC when Jerusalem fell to the Babylonians. The prophesy of Obadiah may be dated shortly after that catastrophe. Edom's part in the fall of Jerusalem is reflected in the Apocrypha. In 1 Esdras 4:45 Edom is charged indirectly with the burning of the Temple when Judah was desolated by the Babylonians.

The Purpose

A twofold purpose dominates the two major sections of Obadiah: (1) to announce judgment upon Edom and (2) to bring comfort and

hope to God's people. Edom's hostile actions against Judah formed
the basis for God's judgment. Judah's hope lay in the promises of
restoration and exaltation.

Indictment of Edom for Hostility
Toward Jacob
1-14

Title (1a)

"The vision of Obadiah" is the title of the book. "Vision" was a
common method of prophetic reception of God's revelation. All that
is contained in Obadiah's book is "vision." Obadiah was a prophet
since he was the recipient of revelation from God. "Thus says the
Lord God concerning Edom" is a secondary title. It marks the book
as a message from God, identifies God as "Yahweh," and names
"Edom" as the nation with whom the message is concerned.

Pride as a Prelude to Edom's Fall (1b-4)

"We have heard tidings from the Lord" may be a reference to the
earlier revelation shared by Obadiah and Jeremiah. Obadiah would
be saying that the earlier prophecy was true. It had been or was
being fulfilled. "Tidings" (that which is heard) is emphatic. "From
the Lord" cites the source of the "tidings." The Lord was alerting
his people to prepare themselves for an emergency. The "messenger" (herald) was sent from Edom "among the nations" to stir them
up for battle against Judah.

"Rise up! let us rise against her for battle!" was the herald's
message. "Her" is taken by most interpreters to be a reference to
Edom, and, thus, the effort made here was to arouse nations to
battle against Edom. Against that interpretation is the fact that the
pronouns related to Edom are consistently masculine in Obadiah.
"Her" probably refers to Judah. Though "Judah" does not stand in
the text here, it may have been in the quoted source.

The Lord alerted his people to the conspiracy of Edom (v. 1b) and went on to comfort Judah with the pledge to deal with Edom (vv. 2-4). God would intervene in Edom's affairs and make Edom "small." The form of the verb translated "I will make" suggests a completed act, or a future one that is so certain that it can be stated as though it had been done already. Edom thought they were great (vv. 3-4); God would make them small. "You shall be utterly despised" is literally "despised [are] you exceedingly."

Edom's root problem was "pride" (v. 3). It was Edom's pride that "deceived" (beguiled) them. They were proud about where they lived, "high" and "in the clefts of the rock." They thought they were absolutely safe there. Edom's pride was reflected in their boast, "Who will bring me down to the ground?"

Edom shared many characteristics of "the eagle" (v. 4). Eagles soar high in the sky and nest "among the stars" (highest peaks). Edom exalted himself and dwelt high in the mountains. Both descended to attack helpless victims. God's answer to Edom's insolent boast is, "I will bring you down."

Prediction of Edom's Complete Devastation (5-9)

With two similar exclamations, the theme of these verses is stated: "how you have been destroyed" (v. 5) and "how Esau has been pillaged" (v. 6). Edom's total destruction is contrasted with two common experiences. "Thieves" and "plunderers" usually steal only "enough for themselves." Normally they don't carry off everything. "Grape gatherers" similarly leave some "gleanings." But Edom has been "destroyed" (cut off) completely.

"Esau," the brother of Jacob (v. 10), identifies Edom with their ancient ancestor (v. 6). "Has been pillaged" means literally "searched." The matching line, "his treasures sought out," indicates the thoroughness with which Edom's hidden treasures would be sought. These treasures would become booty for the invaders.

"Allies," "confederates," and "trusted friends" refer to Edom's allies (v. 7). Loss of all their wealth left Edom impotent (vv. 5-6). To lose all their friends would be utterly devastating. Their allies "deceived" them by making promises and not fulfilling them. All of their "confederates" and "trusted friends" ultimately turned on them. Edom simply could not understand the turn of events.

Edom's blindness to the insincerity of her allies is explained in verse 8. The Lord would "destroy the wise men" and "understanding." "Understanding" is the power to see and estimate things accurately. The loss of wisdom represents another step in Edom's utter desolation.

Even Edom's "mighty men" (warriors, soldiers) could not be counted on to rescue them (v. 9). The verb translated "shall be dismayed" means to be broken. "Teman" was a major city in Edom and the name of a district as well. The reason for the dismay of Edom's soldiers may be seen clearly if the word translated "so that" is translated "because." Their dismay was "because every man from Mount Esau" would be "cut off."

Reasons for Edom's Destruction (10-14)

"By slaughter" (v. 9) and "for the violence" (v. 10) may be two reasons for Edom's destruction (Septuagint). "For slaughter" stands for the personal wrongs Edom inflicted upon Judah. "For the violence" refers to damage done to Judah's religious customs and institutions. "Your brother Jacob" recalls the long-standing feud between Isaac's twin sons, Jacob and Esau. Edom's violence against a family member made it even more reprehensible. "Shame" would cover them. To be "cut off for ever" sounds very final.

Edom's violent attitudes and actions against Judah are enumerated in verses 11-14. While "strangers" looted Judah and Jerusalem, Edom "stood aloof." When "foreigners" divided up the spoils in Jerusalem, Edom acted "like one of them" (v. 11). They "gloated" over Judah's destruction, "rejoiced" over their ruin, and "boasted" in their day of distress (v. 12). They "entered the gate" to gloat and to loot Judah's treasures (v. 13). They "cut off . . . fugitives" (captives) to sell them into slavery (v. 14).

Announcement of the Lord's Recompense upon the Nations
15-18

The judgment upon Edom is set in the larger context of God's general judgment of the nations. What "the day of the Lord" would mean for the foreign nations generally, it would mean to Edom particularly.

Nearness of the Day of the Lord (15-16)

Obadiah's emphases on the day of the Lord include: (1) the nearness of it, (2) the universal implications of it, and (3) the basis of God's intervention. Its nearness should cause "all the nations" to give full attention to preparation for it. Its universal implication ("upon all the nations") should urge each nation to intensify its preparation. And the basis of God's evaluation of the nations should intensify their preparation even more. What Edom had done to others would be done to Edom.

The "you" of verse 16 is Judah. They had "drunk" the wine of God's wrath when the Babylonians came and destroyed them. On the day of the Lord all the nations would "drink" from the cup of God's wrath. The result would be their utter destruction. They would "be as though they had not been."

Escapees of the House of Jacob (17)

"Mount Zion" was associated with the Temple, the place of God's residence in Jerusalem. Foreigners had come and desecrated that revered hill. But in the day of the Lord it would be "holy" again because of God's presence there. For the same reason it would be a place of "escape" for Judah. "The house of Jacob" may include both Israel and Judah here. They would be restored to the Land of Promise, "their own possessions."

No Survivors for Esau (18)

"The house of Jacob" means Judah, and "the house of Joseph" means Israel in verse 18. They would be reunited in restoration to their land and become the instrument of God's wrath upon Edom. The "fire" and "flame" of divine visitation would sweep across Edom, the field of "stubble." Esau would be annihilated.

Return and Restoration of Israel
19-21

All of Israel's old territory would be regained by them in the restoration. Because of the large number of returning exiles new territory would be required.

Expansion of Israel's Territory (19-20)

Israel's old territory had been occupied by Edomites, Philistines, Samaritans, and Ammonites after the fall of Samaria in 722 BC and after the fall of Jerusalem in 587 BC. These territories would be regained by the returning exiles (v. 19). "Halah" was the site of Israel's deportation (2 Kings 17:6). Israel's returning exiles would occupy Phoenician territory "as far as Zarephath" on the Mediterranean coast between Tyre and Sidon (v. 20). "Exiles of Jerusalem" would possess the "Negeb."

Sovereignty of the Lord's Rule (21)

The "saviors" (deliverers) must be the restored exiles of verses 17-19. Contrast is between "Mount Zion," the holy mount, and "Mount Esau," the mount of profanation. Restored Israel would dominate Edom. Finally, Yahweh will rule over all.

JONAH

Introduction

The Book of Jonah reflects the evangelistic spirit of the New Testament better than any other Old Testament book. It is a counterblast to the narrow nationalism, racial exclusiveness, and religious intolerance promoted by Nehemiah and Ezra in the fifth century BC. It is a strong call for Israel to fulfill her vocation to spread the message of God's love and forgiveness to Gentile nations.

The Prophet

A prophet named Jonah (Dove) prophesied during the reign of Jeroboam II (786-746 BC), according to 2 Kings 14:25. That prophet and the one whose ministry is related in the Book of Jonah are often seen to be identical. Jonah's father was named Amittai, and his home was Gath-hepher near Nazareth. Both Jewish and Christian tradition locate a tomb of Jonah at a site identified with ancient Gath-hepher. Jonah predicted correctly that Jeroboam II would recapture from Syria land previously occupied by Israel. God commissioned the prophet to bear a message to Nineveh (1:2; 3:2). But nothing of this mission is mentioned in the Kings material.

The Author

Most modern interpreters agree that the eighth-century prophet named Jonah was not the author of the book that bears his name. With only a few exceptions (1:9; 2:2-9; 4:2,8b,9b), references to Jonah in the book are in the third person. Only the Book of Jonah among the twelve Minor Prophets is a story about the prophet himself. The others are made up largely of prophetic sayings. No one has proposed a name for the author of the Book of Jonah. That he was a pious Jew who understood Israel's mission as the people of God is clear from his writings.

The Date

Obviously date and authorship are tied together. If the Jonah mentioned in 2 Kings 14:25 did not write the book, who did? If it was not written in the eighth century BC, when was it written? It could not have been written earlier than the era associated with the reign of Jeroboam II, nor later than 200 BC. Ecclesiasticus (about 200 BC) refers to "the twelve prophets"; therefore, the Book of Jonah must have been included in the list. The book has some Aramaic words in it, which suggests a date near or after the Exile. Theological concepts in Jonah are related to Jeremiah and the last part of Isaiah. The need was urgent to carry forward their theme of missionary universalism just after the return of the exiles to Jerusalem. A suitable date for the composition of the book would be around 400 BC.

Literary Form

The Book of Jonah is not a collection of prophetic oracles. It is a narrative about a prophet, somewhat like the accounts about Joseph, Elijah, and Ruth. But most interpreters have concluded that the author did not set out to write a historical document. He used the historical, nationalistic Jonah to represent the narrowness, intolerance, and exclusiveness of the returned exiles. The facts that Jonah's name means "dove," and that Hosea compared Israel to a dove (Hos. 7:11), may explain the choice of "Jonah." This story about Jonah has been compared to the parables of Jesus. Its purpose is didactic (intended to teach), but its spirit is prophetic. Jonah 2:2-9 is a hymn of thanksgiving. It is very much like the psalms in the Psalter. The prose of the story is excellent. It is carefully constructed and artfully patterned. It is characterized by action and reaction between the Lord and the prophet.

The Prophet's Rebellion and the Lord's Response
1:1-16

The language of verse 1 marks Jonah as a prophet. Similar words appear in the superscriptions of other prophetic books (Joel 1:1;

Hosea 1:1; Micah 1:1; Ezek. 1:3; Jer. 1:2). How that communication came from God to Jonah is not disclosed. But that he was called to carry a message to Nineveh is stated in verse 2.

Commissioned to Preach (1:1-2)

The conjunction "now" (literally and) at the beginning of verse 1 does not mean that Jonah was originally one in a cycle of stories. Several other Old Testament books begin the same way (1 Sam., Ruth, Ezek.). The usage became customary and does not require the location of an antecedent. "The word of the Lord" means revelation from God. Possible methods of reception of that message include vision, audition, or inner voice. "Jonah the son of Amittai" identifies the recipient as the historical Jonah.

Three sharp commands constitute God's call to the prophet: "Arise," "go," "cry" (v. 2). "Arise" means prepare for service where God may direct. It is a standby command to await orders. "Go to Nineveh" pinpoints the location of his ministry. "Cry against it" may be understood as an order to call, announce, or proclaim some message of judgment upon Nineveh. "For their wickedness has come up before me" is not the content of the prophet's message but the basis of his commission to bear a message from God to them. God was aware of their "wickedness" (evil, calamity).

Rebellion Against the Lord's Call (1:3)

God said "arise." Jonah "rose." However, the appearance of obedience is quickly dispelled. The translation of the conjunction as "but" interprets the prophet's response as rebellion. He got up and went, but he went the wrong way. His purpose in rising was "to flee" in rebellion. The Lord's "presence" made him uncomfortable because his spirit was not in tune with God's Spirit. "Tarshish," his destination, was in the opposite direction from "Nineveh," God's destination for him. Jonah thought he could escape from God in Tarshish.

"Joppa" was the nearest port to Jonah. His going "down" to Joppa was Jonah's first step in a series of downhill moves. He went "down" to Joppa, "down" into the inner part of the ship, "down" into sleep, and ultimately down into the sea. Every step was aimed at escaping "the presence of the Lord" (vv. 3,5,10,15). Several mining towns on the Mediterranean Sea were named Tarshish. Perhaps it was located in Spain and represented in Jonah's mind the city most distant from his own land. At the same time it would put the greatest distance possible between him and Nineveh.

Response to the Prophet's Rebellion (1:4-16)

God's reaction to Jonah's rebellion is implied by the conjunction "but" (v. 4). God initiated. Jonah moved. God made a countermove. For emphasis, "the Lord" is placed in front of the verb "hurled." The "great wind" was subject to his control. With it, God created "a mighty tempest," that is, a raging storm. To say the word is to make the sound of the wind as it shrieked past the sails. The ship's response to the sudden storm is pictured graphically. For emphasis "ship" is put first in the sentence. The ship's struggle is portrayed in the following literal translation: "the ship thought to be broken up."

The radical response of the sailors reveals the severity of the storm (v. 5). Fear gripped these seasoned sailors, and they prayed and worked. "Each" is literally "a man." "Cried" is not from the word rendered "cry" in Jonah's commission. The term here is descriptive of a cry of distress addressed in prayer to God. The phrase, "each cried to his god," implies a variety of pagan deities. These tough but scared sailors added work to their prayers. They followed a common practice in the fact of a storm at sea of casting overboard all nonessentials. Their purpose was to "lighten" the load in order to make the ship ride higher on the waves. Thereby they hoped to avoid being swamped.

Jonah's sleep in the midst of a mighty tempest may be explained by the form of the verb translated "had gone down" (v. 5b). The implication is that he had gone down into the inner part of the ship before the storm came up. His struggle with the call of God left him physically, mentally, and emotionally exhausted. That would explain his desire to find a secluded retreat on board the ship where sleep might silence God's disturbing call. "Was fast asleep" has the root idea of falling into a heavy sleep. The same root is used in Genesis 2:21 to describe Adam's deep sleep when God removed a sidepiece from him to make the woman. The conjunction "but" suggests that Jonah's going down into the ship and his falling into a deep sleep were part of his rebellious flight from God.

"Captain" comes from two words: a basic word for sailor which means rope twister and another term that means "great," or "chief." The combination means literally "the great (chief) rope twister." He it was who "came" (approached) and awakened Jonah from his sleep and to the danger. The captain's question indicates that he found Jonah's deep sleep in the face of the raging storm incredible. Literally his question is "What to you being in deep sleep?" Again Jonah heard the command "Arise." This time it came from a pagan ship captain ordering him to pray to the very God who had ordered him to go to Nineveh. "Call" here means seek an audience with God in prayer. That same word in his commission meant announce God's message. The sailors had prayed but to no avail. Perhaps Jonah's God was the one who expressed his wrath in the storm. The definite article attached to the generic word for God ("god") may suggest the captain's belief in a supreme deity. His hope in ordering Jonah to pray was that Jonah's God might "give a thought" (show himself gracious) and save them from perishing in the storm.

By casting lots the sailors wanted to discover who among them was responsible for their plight (v. 7). The lot fell on guilty Jonah. At every turn in the story God's providential control is magnified. Some uncertainty of the outcome is implied in the form of the verb rendered "that we may know." "Evil" means calamity, not moral evil. When the lot fell on Jonah, the sailors sought through questioning to get a confession of guilt from him (v. 8). The lot said Jonah was the culprit, but they wanted him to confess it. "Tell us" (declare to us) is a command, but it is softened by a particle of entreaty meaning "we pray," or "please." In fairness they offered Jonah an opportunity to defend himself. His answers to their five questions would either confirm or deny the decision by lot. They asked him to admit his guilt, give his business on the ship, tell his origin, indicate his country, and identify his family.

Jonah's answer revealed his racial (national) identity and his religious beliefs (v. 9). "Hebrew" is placed in the emphatic position in the sentence. It is the term Abraham's descendants used when identifying themselves to foreigners (Gen. 40:15; Ex. 2:7). "I fear the Lord" does not mean "I am afraid of Yahweh." It designates a worshiper, one who reverences the Lord. How ironical that Jonah was fleeing in defiant disobedience to Yahweh's overt command! "The God of heaven" indicates the Lord's supreme majesty. This one worshiped by Jonah was the Creator. He made "the sea," now churned into tempestuous terror in response to Jonah's rebellious flight from God. He also made "the dry land" on which Jonah should have been hastening toward Nineveh to fulfill God's calling.

At first, the mariners were afraid of the storm (v. 5). Now they were afraid of God (v. 10). "Then the men were exceedingly afraid" is literally "then the men feared a great fear." These rugged sailors were reduced to fear and a sense of their frailty before the tempest hurled into the sea by the Creator to arrest his fleeing prophet. The word rendered "afraid" was used in verse 9 to describe Jonah as one who reverenced God. "What is this that you have done!" refers to the sailors' knowledge that Jonah was running from God. Apparently he gave that information as the basis for requesting passage on their ship. But until the storm and the lot casting to determine guilt, they had dismissed Jonah's religious motive for boarding their ship. Now the pieces of the puzzle fit together to reveal that the storm really was on Jonah's account.

The situation was desperate so far as the sailors were concerned. Something had to be done, but they wanted to be fair to Jonah. Their question of what to do to him is a request for his suggestion and counsel (v. 11). After all it was a matter between Jonah and his God. Jonah should know the ritual requirement for appeasing his angry God. The growing intensity of the storm put urgency into their question. "For the sea grew more and more tempestuous" is literally "for the sea was walking and raging." Use of two participles here reveals the continuous growth in the storm's intensity.

Jonah's response to the sailor's question contains an acknowledge-ment of guilt and a willingness to accept the punishment due him (v. 12). His instruction to "take me up" and "throw me into the sea" may not be as noble as some interpreters have imagined. This may represent his willingness to die in a watery grave rather than preach to the hated Ninevites. Nothing short of Jonah's removal from the ship would silence the sea. The continuous walking and raging of the sea caused the knowledge of Jonah's guilt to be pressed in upon him continuously.

At first, the sailors refused to cast Jonah overboard, preferring to put forth every effort humanly possible to save him from such a death and save themselves from the storm (v. 13). The verb translated "rowed hard" means literally "dug." But the raging storm nullified their noble efforts. Before following Jonah's advice the sailors prayed. "Cried" is from the verb usually translated "call." It means call upon the Lord in prayer here, as the particle of entreaty, "we beseech thee," indicates. Their request was that they not "perish" for Jonah's "life" (soul) and that God not "lay" (give, set) innocent blood upon them. They were not claiming innocence for Jonah before his God. They were simply pointing out that the prophet had done nothing to deserve death at their hands.

The mariners acknowledged the absolute sovereignty of God (v. 14b). Whatever he pleased to do he did. He sent the storm. He controlled the lot. For the sailors to cast Jonah into the sea would only be the carrying out of God's good pleasure. They had covered all the bases in an effort to protect themselves from the wrath of God. Then they proceeded to follow Jonah's counsel. They "threw him into the sea" (v. 15), and it "ceased from its raging." "Ceased" is from a verb that means to stand or stay. The change of the sea from boisterous to balmy must have been immediate and dramatic.

Could it be that "the men," who had responded with fear to the storm (v. 5) and to the Lord (v. 10), now responded with reverence to God (v. 16)? The language is the same here as in verse 10, except for the addition here of "the Lord." Their offering of sacrifice and making of vows implies worship and reverence for God. "Offered a sacrifice" and "made vows" is literally "sacrificed a sacrifice" and "vowed vows" respectively. God's acceptance of the prayers, sacrifice, and vows of these foreign sailors demonstrated that true worship of God was not limited to Israel (as to people) nor Jerusalem (as to place). Pagans could respond to the mercy and grace of God.

The Prophet's Prayer and the Lord's Response
1:17 to 2:10

Jonah 1:17 in the Revised Standard Version is Jonah 2:1 in the Hebrew text. To handle it as the beginning of chapter 2 gives an opening divine action to match the closing one in 2:10.

Swallowed by a Fish (1:17)

The pattern of move and countermove between the Lord and Jonah is continued in this verse. Yahweh acted to save Jonah from sure death in the sea. "Appointed" is the translation of a verb whose root idea is to count, number, or reckon. It does not designate a special creative act of God. The implication is that God selected an existing "fish" to serve a special purpose. "Fish" is a generic noun. It may denote a variety of great sea monsters, including the whale and the shark. It was a "great" (large) fish selected "to swallow up Jonah."

The form of the verb rendered "swallow" suggests selection for a specific purpose. Some interpreters suggest that the writer deliberately made a reference to a prophecy in Jeremiah 51:34 and 44 about Israel being swallowed by Babylon and then delivered. Only by divine intervention could a man be kept alive and unharmed in the belly of a fish for "three days and three nights." Israel's restoration from captivity in Babylon was a similar miracle. Jesus quoted this verse as an illustration of his ministry (Matt. 12:39-41; Luke 11:29-32).

Prayer for Deliverance (2:1-9)

Verse 1 contains the announcement that Jonah prayed; verses 2-9 purport to give the prayer. The tone of the prayer is more of thanksgiving after the fact of deliverance than appeal in the midst of desperate circumstances. This psalm has close affinities with other psalms in the Psalter. It may have been taken from hymns used to express gratitude for deliverance from Exile.

God moved to appoint a great fish to swallow up Jonah. Jonah prayed, apparently for deliverance (v. 9). But an appropriate question to ask is, From what did Jonah ask to be delivered? The answer in the hymn of thanksgiving set in this context is deliverance from death by drowning. Jonah had asked to die in the depths of the sea as a final act of his rebellious flight from God's call. Faced with the prospect of death, the prophet thanked God for deliverance by the fish. It was from "the deep," "the flood," "thy waves," "thy billows," "the waters," and "weeds" that Jonah prayed for deliverance.

The verb forms in the psalm indicate completed action and, thus, past activities. "Called" is from the same verb used to express the sailors' prayer in 1:14. Jonah prayed to the very God from whom he fled (v. 2). The root idea in the term translated "distress" is restrict. Jonah was in a tight spot. But God was open and attentive to the prayers of his rebel prophet. He "answered" Jonah's distress call. In the poetic parallelism here "distress" and "Sheol" are synonymous.

"Sheol" was the abode of the dead. The "belly of Sheol" means near the gates of death. Even from there God heard Jonah's "voice" (prayer).

The prophet felt abandoned, forsaken, cast off by his God (v. 3). "Deep" may refer either to the depths of the sea or to deep distress. "Heart of the seas," "the flood" (river), "thy waves," and "thy billows" indicate that "deep" refers to the depths of the sea. Even so the basic feeling of the poet is that he has been abandoned by God (v. 4). To emphasize the personal pain associated with being "cast out," a separate first-person pronoun is used in addition to the first-person pronoun indicated in the verb form. A free rendering would be, "I, even I, said I am cast out." "From thy presence" is literally "from opposite your eyes."

The adverb translated "how" (RSV) should be rendered "yet" (v. 4b). Everything about Jonah's distressful circumstances implied that he was "cast out" from the presence of God. Even so he would "again look" to God's "holy temple," contrary to what he might be expected to do under the circumstances. The Temple must have been the one the returning exiles built. It had become the center of worship. Toward it the Jews looked when they prayed (Dan. 6:10).

The phrase "closed in over me" is literally "encompassed unto life [soul]" (v. 5). "Deep" is not from the word translated "deep" in verse 3. It is the term used to designate the primeval ocean in Genesis 1:2. Here it designates the subterranean waters in contrast with the "waters" of ordinary seas. With each additional line, Jonah's distress deepens. "Weeds" grow at the bottom of the sea, that is, "the roots of the mountains." To go down to "the land whose bars closed upon me forever" means either to enter Sheol never to return, or to die in a watery grave with no hope of returning to dry land.

But the poet's testimony is that from the deepest and darkest distress, even from the "Pit" God caused his "life" to go up. Frequently in poetry "Pit" is set in a parallel position to "Sheol." It was Yahweh, the poet's personal God, who saved his life from the Pit. It was when his "soul [life] fainted" (was overwhelmed) that he remembered Yahweh (v. 7). "The Lord" is made emphatic by its position before the verb. The emphasis is preserved in a literal translation "the Lord I remembered." With memory of the Lord came a reminder of who God was and what he had done in the past and could do now. "Prayer" naturally followed remembrance. To say that his prayer "came" to God in his "holy temple" means that his prayer gained an audience with the Almighty. God heard his prayer.

The words translated "vain idols" means practically the same thing (v. 8). Literally the words are "lying vanities." They are empty nothings, nonentities. To "pay regard" to such is to trust in that which can offer no help. And to do that is to "forsake their true loyalty." Sometimes the word translated "true loyalty" is rendered "loving-kindness." It is the term for covenant love and loyalty.

Appropriately, "but" is used to point up the contrast between the idolators of verse 8 and the true worshipers in verse 9. The emphatic "I" sharpens the contrast. "Thanksgiving" should be the pervasive mood of "sacrifice." Sacrifice was prescribed and required, but vows were voluntary. In reference to Jonah the paying of vows would mean obedience to God. The psalm ends on a triumphant note, "Deliverance [salvation] belongs to the Lord!" Jonah's salvation and Israel's deliverance from Exile in Babylon both came from God.

Answer to the Prophet's Prayer (2:10)

The Lord had "appointed a great fish to swallow up Jonah" (1:17). Jonah prayed a prayer of thanksgiving for saving him from a watery grave (2:1). Then the Lord "spoke" (literally "said") to the fish. In obedience to God's instruction, the fish "vomited out Jonah upon the dry land" (v. 10). Jonah ran from God in rebellion. Then he ran to God in repentance. He was in position again to hear and obey God's commission.

The Prophet's Obedience and the Lord's Response
3:1-10

When Jonah repented, God gave him a second chance to obey the call to service. When Jonah obeyed the call to service, God gave Nineveh a chance to repent. When Nineveh repented, God repented of the evil he had announced against them.

Faithful Proclamation of the Message (3:1-4)

A second call experience is not uncommon among the prophets. Hosea was called to "take . . . a wife" (1:2). Later, after she had left him, God called him to "Go again, love a woman" (3:1). His call to prophetic ministry and his call to take a wife were tied together intimately, but this is not quite the same as Jonah's second call. The only difference between the introductory statements to Jonah's two call accounts is that where Jonah 1:1 has "the son of Amittai," Jonah 3:1 has "the second time." The fact that God calls a man to service speaks volumes about God's method and purpose. A second call to the same man reveals his persistence, forbearance, and mercy. One of the great lessons of the Book of Jonah is that God gives a second chance. If the prophet represents the nation, then this second call is a second chance for Israel to fulfill her high calling of missionary service.

The commission here in 3:2 is almost identical to the first call (1:2). In each case, where he should preach and the source of his message are made crystal clear. Nineveh was the place, and God was the source. The verb translated "proclaim" in 3:2 was rendered "cry" in 1:2. At first Jonah was commissioned to "cry against it." The second time he was charged to "proclaim to it." But the prepositions "against" and "to" are used interchangeably. The real differences in the two calls are in the last lines: "for their wickedness has come up before me" (1:2) and "the message that I tell you" (3:2). "Message" is from the same root as "proclaim" and to reveal the relationship might be translated "proclaim the proclamation." With a participle, present and continuous action is indicated. "That I tell you" is literally "which I am speaking unto you." God was supplying the message in the moment of his call to Jonah. Apparently it was the message Jonah preached in Nineveh, namely, "Yet forty days, and Nineveh shall be overthrown!" (v. 4).

Jonah's response to the second call was radically different from his response to the first call. Notice the contrast: "But Jonah rose to flee to Tarshish from the presence of the Lord" (1:3); "So Jonah arose [same words in Hebrew to this point] and went to Nineveh, according to the word of the Lord" (3:3). The two responses are as different as rebellion and obedience. Positive response to God's call to go to Nineveh may have been part of Jonah's vow (2:9).

Inclusion of the verb "was," when in Hebrew usage that verb

often is understood (and thus not written), plus the form of the verb
(completed action) may indicate that Nineveh was no longer a "great
city" (v. 3b). "Three days journey in breath" is literally "walking
three days." That either means that the designation "Nineveh"
included nearby towns and villages, or that the ministry of
proclamation in the whole city would take three days. "An exceedingly great city" is actually "a city great to [for] God" and lends
support to the second suggestion. Though it was pagan and corrupt,
it belonged to God. Its inhabitants were accountable to God. They
needed the message of God. Without it, they were doomed. That is
why Jonah's ministry was so urgent and so critical.

The verb translated "began" has the root idea of untie, or loosen,
associated with it. Jonah's entering the city on a mission for God
means that he was free from his former rebellion. He was no longer
restricted from service by his former prejudice against Nineveh. "To
go" means "to enter" (come). "Going a day's journey" is literally
"walking one day." This phrase probably designates one day of the
prophet's ministry of preaching in Nineveh, not a twenty-mile trek
(the distance a man could walk in one day). Jonah's message was a
brief five words (Hebrew) in length: "Yet forty days, and Nineveh
shall be overthrown" (eight words in English).

Jonah's pointed message was not popular, but it was powerful. The
response of the people of Nineveh reveals how effective his sermon
really was. Jonah was the instrument God used to deliver the
message. But the emphasis falls on the message, not the messenger.
It was a prediction of Nineveh's impending destruction. It was a
message devoid of an expressed hope. And yet the people must have
understood as the prophet did that Nineveh might be spared by
repentance.

Faith Response of the People (3:5-9)

"The people of Nineveh believed God" is an astounding statement (v. 5a). "People" is actually "men," the same word used to
refer to the sailors (1:10,16). "Believed God" is literally "believed in
God." An inseparable preposition is attached to the word for God to
mark the object of belief. "Believed" comes from a verb that means
confirm, support, verify in its basic form. But it means stand firm,
trust, or believe in the form used here. Evidence is lacking that

Nineveh's response to Jonah's message produced lasting results. Even so the author's lesson that God's love extends to pagan nations stands firm.

To demonstrate their sincere response to Jonah's preaching, the people of Nineveh "proclaimed a fast" (v. 5*b*). The basic meaning of the verb translated "proclaimed" is "call." Here the word means announce or proclaim. The external signs of fasting included the wearing of "sackcloth." All the people of Nineveh participated in the fast, old and young, great and small. What a contrast between Nineveh's prompt obedience to God's word and Jonah's earlier disobedience!

The "king of Nineveh" joined his subjects in fasting when he heard the "tidings" of Jonah's message (v. 6). "Tidings" is literally "the word" (the matter, or the thing). Perhaps what the king heard was both Jonah's shattering sermon and the people's singular response. At any rate he humbled himself by removing his royal robe, donning sackcloth, and sitting in ashes. These outward gestures demonstrated his sincere repentance. The root meaning of the verb translated "And he made proclamation" is "cry," or "cry out" in need, or in distress (v. 7*a*). But the form of the verb here means "to have proclamation made." The verb rendered "published" is literally "said."

The king and his "nobles" (great ones) sent out a "decree" that both "man" (mankind) and "beast" were to refrain from eating and drinking (v. 7*b*). A word play is evident here. The noun rendered "decree" and the verb translated "taste" are derived from the same verbal root. Even the animals were to be included in the wearing of sackcloth (v. 8*a*). But the king instructed his people to add prayer and turning from "evil" and "violence" to their fasting. "Every one" is literally "a man" (individual person). "Let them cry mightily to God" is literally "let them call unto God with strength." True repentance is more than observance of rituals. It is a radical change in life. It is putting off "evil" and "violence," not merely putting on sackcloth and sitting in ashes.

The king's decree did not presume upon God. "Who knows" means perhaps (v. 9). The one true God (the definite article is attached to the noun for God) may "repent" (relent) and "turn" from his burning anger. If Nineveh would turn from evil, God might turn away his judgment. In that case the Ninevites would not "perish."

Final Action of the Lord (3:10)

God observed "what they did," not what they said or what rituals they performed (v. 10). What they did that pleased God was turn "from their evil way." "Evil way" means immoral life-style. When God observed the radical change in the Ninevites, he "repented" (breathed a sigh of relief). He did not do the "evil" he "said" (spoke) he would do to them. "Evil" here means the calamitous destruction of Nineveh (3:4). God's grace and mercy were extended to pagan people based on their repentance and faith. This should have served as a sharp rebuke of Israel's exclusiveness.

The Prophet's Resentment and the Lord's Response
4:1-11

The moves and countermoves between Jonah and God are evident in this final chapter. Jonah preached. Nineveh repented. God relented. Disaster for Nineveh was averted. But Jonah did not rejoice over the fact that Nineveh escaped the announced judgment. Did his displeasure reflect his prejudice against Nineveh, or was he concerned that he might be discredited as a prophet? Whatever Jonah's reason for being displeased, God was displeased with Jonah.

Resentment over Nineveh's Repentance (4:1-4)

Usually a messenger of God will rejoice when the message he bears is met by a positive response. But that was not Jonah's reaction. The root meaning of the verb rendered "displeased" is "be evil," or "be bad." A noun built on the verb is translated "evil" as a general rule. But in combination with the verb meaning "be evil" and with the adjective "great" controlling the noun here, it means "displeased exceedingly." "And he was angry" is literally "and it burned for him." He was hot over the response of the Ninevites.

Jonah's prayer is not a show of his piety and devotion (v. 2). Bitter resentment is in every word of it. Chapter 1 has no reference to an exchange between the Lord and Jonah that included the subject of Jonah's prayer here in verses 1-3. But some such argument with God must have preceded his flight to Tarshish. Though Jonah's message contained no hint of a conditional nature about it, he knew the nature of God. He knew if Nineveh repented God would spare them. His prayer is an effort at self-justification. He fled at first because he did not want to be the means of warning Nineveh and thereby making possible their escape from God's judgment.

Jonah's description of the nature of God is similar to the list of attributes found in other contexts in the Old Testament (Ex. 34:6 ff.; Ps. 86:15; Joel 2:13; Mic. 7:18). "Gracious" means the bestowal of unmerited favor. "Merciful" means intimate compassion of the kind existing between a mother and her child, or between brothers. "Slow to anger" implies that God is long on patience. "Abounding in steadfast love" describes the overflowing loyal love of God in the convenant relationship. "Repentest of evil" suggests that God breathes a sigh of relief when his announced calamity upon people can be averted.

Jonah was so distraught over the turn of events that he asked to die (v. 3). The word translated "therefore" is normally rendered "now." Jonah's request that Yahweh "take" his life acknowledges that Yahweh is the giver of life and that he alone has the authority to take life. It was not Jonah's prerogative to take his own life. Jonah's jaded view is indicated by his statement, "'it is better for me to die than to live'."

The Lord's question to Jonah is left unanswered (v. 4). Later, in another interview, Jonah gave a positive answer to a similar question (v. 9). But here Yahweh's question is met with silence. Perhaps no answer was needed or expected. The Lord simply wanted Jonah to consider whether or not his anger was justified.

Rebuke for the Prophet's Narrowness (4:5-11)

Jonah left God's question unanswered, broke off the interview with God, and left the city (v. 5). He built a "booth" on the east side of the city to protect himself from the heat of the day and from the chill of the night. Then he sat under the booth in the shade to see what would happen to the city. Jonah chose the "east" side because it would give him an elevated view of Nineveh. Some time lapse is implied between verses 5 and 6. Jonah's need for "a plant" to shade him from the hot sun must have been because the leaves of his temporary booth withered (v. 6). The one who "appointed a great fish" also "appointed a plant." With the fish God rescued Jonah from a watery grave. With the plant he granted Jonah respite from the heat of the sun ("from his evil" literally). Jonah's attention was diverted from the city to the plant. He was glad over the plant, greatly glad. His gladness over a personal comfort should be seen in contrast with his sadness over Nineveh's repentance.

God's sovereignty is revealed in his selection and use of a fish (1:17), then a plant (4:6), next a worm (4:7), and finally a wind (4:8). The worm "attacked" (smote) the plant, and it "withered." Suddenly Jonah's shade was gone. But his trouble had just begun. With the next sunrise, God's "appointed" east wind (sirocco) made Jonah "faint." What made the "east wind" so oppressive was the combination of heat and dust. "Cover" is the root meaning of the verb translated "faint." The form of the verb means "enwrap oneself." That phrase equals "swoon away." In extreme physical and mental distress, Jonah again asked to die. "He asked that he might die" is literally "he asked his soul [life] to die." He concluded that he would be better off dead than alive.

God proceeded to apply the object lessons afforded by the "appointed" plant, worm, and wind. First he raised the question about Jonah's anger over the sudden destruction of the plant. It is a question of attitude and of justification for such an attitude. It is the same question God raised with Jonah about his anger when God did not destroy Nineveh according to Jonah's prediction. To that question Jonah made no response. But to this one he replied, "'I do well to be angry, angry enough to die'" (v. 9b). How absurd that Jonah felt justified in being so angry over the destruction of a mere plant!

Observe the contrasts between the concerns of Jonah (v. 10) and the concerns of God (v. 11). In direct address to Jonah God put Jonah's attitude in perspective. The emphatic "you" referring to Jonah (v. 10) is matched by the emphatic "I" referring to God (v. 11). Jonah looked with compassion upon an insignificant plant. Should not God look with compassion upon the great city of Nineveh? Jonah's "pity" was for a plant which he did not labor to make or cause to grow large. God's "pity" was for people and animals he created and caused to multiply. Jonah's pity was for a plant that "came into being in a night, and perished in a night." It gave only fleeting pleasure. But Nineveh with its teeming population held the potential of giving permanent delight to their Creator.

The "hundred and twenty thousand persons who do not know their right hand from their left" have been identified as children who were not morally responsible. If that interpretation is correct, the total population of Nineveh would have been about six hundred thousand. An alternate approach makes the hundred twenty thousand the total population, a more credible figure to most interpreters. In this interpretation, the phrase "who do not know" refers to the whole city which had not received the moral instruction Israel was commanded to share. The multitude of "cattle" were of more value than a mere plant.

The book ends with an unanswered question. Obviously "yes" is the expected answer. God was certainly justified in showing pity for such a great city. Jonah hated Nineveh. God loved Nineveh. Jonah wanted to see the city destroyed. God wanted to see the city saved. Jonah would have confined God's love and salvation to Israel. God would extend his love and salvation to a pagan people. The rebuke of Jonah was a rebuke of Israel whom he represented. As God gave Jonah a second chance to fulfill his calling as a prophet, so the nation was offered a second chance to fulfill their missionary role to the nations.